THE WICCAN WEB

THE

WICCAN WEB

SURFING THE
MAGIC ON THE INTERNET

PATRICIA TELESCO
and
SIRONA KNIGHT

CITADEL PRESS
Kensington Publishing Corp.
www.kensingtonbooks.com

CITADEL PRESS books are published by

Kensington Publishing Corp.
850 Third Avenue
New York, NY 10022

Illustrations by Colleen Koziara

All Kensington titles, imprints, and distributed lines are available at special quantity discounts for bulk purchases for sales promotions, premiums, fund-raising, educational, or institutional use. Special book excerpts or customized printings can also be created to fit specific needs. For details, write or phone the office of the Kensington special sales manager: Kensington Publishing Corp., 850 Third Avenue, New York, NY 10022, attn: Special Sales Department, phone 1-800-221-2647.

Citadel Press logo Reg. U.S. Patent and Trademark Office
Citadel Press is a trademark of Kensington Publishing Corp.

First printing April 2001

10 9 8 7 6 5 4 3 2 1

Printed in the United States of America

ISBN 0-8065-2197-X

Cataloging-in-Publication data may be obtained from the Library of Congress.

This book is dedicated to my husband, Michael, and my son, Sky, the two computer geniuses in our family. Thank you both for making my cyber life much brighter.

—Sirona Knight

This book, by its subject matter alone, must first be dedicated to the many people in my web (including my coauthor) who have given me much joy, strength, vision, and support over the last ten years. Thank you for letting me live my dream. On a more personal level, this book is dedicated to my Tribe, who I hold close to my heart. I know you all will understand what I mean and appreciate it when I say: "Damn, Talyn!"

Love, Laughter, and Light,

—Patricia Telesco

CONTENTS

ACKNOWLEDGMENTS

The authors would especially like to thank each other for their friendship, without which this book would only be a cyber dream. Many thanks and brightest blessings to our editor, Colette Russen—you rock, Col! Warmest regards and thanks to Colleen Koziara for adding the artist's touch to our work. We would also like to thank Sirona's agent, Lisa Hagan at Paraview, for her support, integrity, and friendship. We would like to respectfully thank Steven Zacharius at Kensington Publishing for publishing this innovative book. We would also like to thank Bruce Bender and Margaret Wolf, also at Kensington, for their continued help and enthusiasm.

Sirona would like to give many thanks and heartfelt appreciation to her family and friends. She would also like to thank everyone of the College of the Sun in Chico, California, for sharing in the Great Adventure. Also grateful thanks to everyone at *Magical Blend* magazine, especially Michael Langevin, the editor and publisher.

Thanks to Skye Alexander, Dorothy Morrison, A. J. Drew, Raven Grimassi, R. J. and Josephine Stewart, and Timothy Roderick for their empowering friendship, and for helping the circle grow ever stronger. And many loving thanks to all of you who send us such great e-mail and chat with us on the Wiccan Web. May the Cyber Goddess and God bless, guide, and protect your every click. So be it! Blessed be!

Introduction: Merry Meet

Yesterday's magic has become today's reality. Through the wonders of technology we're able to accomplish things that our ancestors only dreamed of, from watching events live on television as they occur to exploring space. One of the most far-reaching innovations affecting our culture today both spiritually and substantively is the Internet. Suddenly people from all around the world are networking over vast distances through assemblies made of plastic, metal, and wire. Wiccans have begun to reconnect with our magical tribe in wonderful, educational, and powerful ways.

For example, if a member of the magical community has any pressing need for help or information, she can go online to ask for support. Within hours of hearing about that need, people on the Web are reaching out and offering advice and aid. This means that the Internet represents far more than a method of communication: it's a community support system, a spiritual lifeline, and it holds tremendous potential for magic if we get past the bits 'n bytes long enough to see the possibilities. The use of the Internet provides virtually unlimited possibilities for Wiccans with access to it.

The Wiccan Web was written with this vast potential in mind. For those reading this who think that technology and magic are better left as separate entities, think again. Computers are like demigods in a box. They run on energy, store vast amounts of knowledge, and seem to have persnickety tendencies all their own. This demigod has a quintessential servant: the Internet. The Internet creates lines through which the computer's energy, data, and messages flow. Since by definition magic bends, changes, and redirects energy, it's easy to see that we can transmit that power using the Internet and our computer as the medium (or channeler)!

Seem far-fetched? We're willing to bet by the time you're finished with this book that you won't think so. The Internet is a mirror of the universe, showing us that we are all connected together, and it is our connections to one another that make us whole. As authors of this book, we use the Internet for magical research, to stay in touch with magical friends, to honor sacred powers, and to perform other magical functions every day. In fact, this book was written using the Internet because we live far apart—in New York and California!

Both us believe that our lives would be far more difficult without the conveniences and magical potential the Web offers. This book presents a sample of the ways in which we have brought technology and magic together in the real world and have made it function effectively and successfully—ways that you can easily adapt and apply too.

In this book, you'll learn about designing a computer altar, and about creating a sacred space where that desk or table becomes the focal point for raising and directing power. Next, we'll explore all kinds of spells, rituals, and divination techniques designed to keep your computer system running smoothly, as well as those spells that use computers or computer parts as symbolic components to focus a spell for specific goals. And you'll even learn "Wicca Speak," a fantastic new shorthand symbol-language for Internet communication designed especially for Web Witches!

Finally, to direct you on your way toward successful Web Witching, in chapter 7 we have provided a listing of several Pagan-related Web sites for your exploration. The site information includes the name, URL, and a brief description of the site. We have created sites just for updates and additions to this listing at www.dcsi.net/~bluesky and www.sironaknight.com.

Exploring these Web sites and the links they offer has many benefits. You can learn new magical techniques or theories, network with people of a like mind, investigate areas of personal spiritual interest, find quality goods and services, research multicultural correspondences for animals, crystals, and plants to enrich your Book of Shadows, and much more! So prepare to begin an adventure where technology and magic work hand in hand. Personal and planetary transformation starts here and now by simply turning the page. Blessed Be!

THE WICCAN WEB

1

THE ESSENTIALS

Like any worthwhile endeavor, Web Witching takes some creativity and a little bit of know-how. Despite the fact that most people today are familiar with computer software and applications, not everyone is Web literate or completely at ease surfing the vast sea of Internet technology. The purpose of this chapter is to get you better acquainted with many Internet functions including e-mail, search engines, and protective measures you can take to safeguard your computer from viruses.

The magical element has been left out of this section because we believe that it is best to tackle the mundane necessities of Web Witching before launching into spiritual matters. Think of this chapter as you would the personal preparations you make physically before a ritual. You make sure you are clean, in the right mindset, and well rested, right? Well, your computer needs to be properly set up with sufficient memory and proper energy levels to function efficiently too. By following the suggestions in this chapter and setting up your system accordingly, you will eliminate most of the things that could cause hang-ups, glitches, crashes, or bugs in your system and your magic later on.

Those of you reading this who already have your systems up and running, and who regularly use the Internet, can probably forego this chapter. However, Internet software and capacities change rapidly. What was considered cutting edge last year is literally more than two years out of date now because it was already outdated by the time it hit the market! We recommend skimming the following pages anyway just to see if we've found some worthwhile ideas and information that you might have missed.

Computer System Guidelines and Requirements

By its nature, Web Witching means getting online and extending your magical energy through the lines of force represented by the Internet. If you're not set up to go online yet, this section will give you some good advice on how to start.

To get yourself and your computer ready for Web Witching, first you'll need certain types of hardware and software. If your computer system doesn't have the things we suggest here, shop around and watch the newspaper. Remember: Modems and Internet software can be added to even older systems if they have sufficient memory. So don't let the prices on "hot" technology dissuade you. There are ways to get hooked up and surfing without spending your entire nest egg.

Basic System for Connecting to the Wiccan Web

Computer components you will need to connect to the Internet include a processor and monitor, memory, a hard drive with available disk space, a modem, keyboard, and preferably a disk drive. These components are usually included in any system on the market today. If you do purchase your computer components separately, make sure they are all compatible.

PROCESSOR Your computer processor is the main part of the computer that runs everything else. Processors are rated by how fast the processor can move bits of information to different parts of the system. A 133MHz processor moves these bits around at 133 mega-hertz, and a 200MHz processor moves at 200 megahertz. The higher the number, the faster the computer is able to process the information coming into it.

The faster your processor, the faster Web pages will load on your system, and the faster you will see them on your screen. As far as minimum requirements for connecting to the Internet, Sirona knows several people who do use their old 486 systems for access to the Internet, but they experience glitches (and even crashes) in their systems from time to time. Trish uses a Pentium 133MHz processor, which is by no means fast in terms of what's out there nowadays, but at the same time, it is more than adequate for navigating the Web.

The idea is to find a system that works for you, and update it as your needs increase and prices drop. Don't feel compelled to update every time technology comes up with something new. Waiting usu-ally means you can get a newer system at a much better price.

MONITOR   The price of your computer monitor depends largely on the size of the screen. Bigger screens are easier to see but are more expensive. Sirona uses a standard fifteen-inch VGA monitor, which is a little on the small side, especially as the prices of seventeen-inch monitors continue to drop. The thing about larger monitors is that they save on your eyesight, making the investment worthwhile in terms of your health, particularly if you spend large amounts of time in front of your computer. The Web is a very visual place, and with a larger monitor, you'll be able to see more of a Web docu-ment at one time than with a smaller screen.

Space is another factor that comes into play when selecting a monitor. Bigger monitors take up more space on your desk. All told, the bottom line comes down to buying the monitor that meets your needs and pocketbook.

MEMORY AND DISK SPACE   The terms *memory* and *disk space* are often thought of as being interchangeable, when in fact they are two dis-tinct things. Memory has to do with how many memory chips are in your processor or motherboard, usually expressed in terms of megabites (MB) of RAM. What these megabites of RAM do is allow you to do more than one task at a time. The more tasks you want to do, the more megs of RAM you need. Programs such as Windows stay resident in your computer's memory at all times, and thus require memory. As computer software evolves, so does its need for memory. Previously you could run everything under Windows just fine with 16 MB of RAM, but now that number is up to about 64 MB, and steadily rising. One of the things you can do when buying a new system is make sure you can add more memory later as your needs increase. Adding memory chips is usually not difficult and relatively inexpensive.

Disk space has to do with the amount of space you have on your hard drive for the storage of information. Unlike memory, which is running all the time, disk space comes into play when you save a document or load new software programs onto your computer's hard drive. There are two main reasons it is important to have sufficient disk space when you go on the Internet: First, the software available for connecting to and surfing the Web takes up a fair amount of disk space, depending on the program(s) you load; and second, the Web software, also known as your browser, creates temporary files and history files that are constantly being stored and updated on your computer's hard drive. In this way, sufficient disk space is an important component to going on the Web. Sirona's hard drive has 30.0 gigabytes (GB), and this has been more than enough for surfing the Internet and downloading programs without worrying about running out of space on her hard drive. New systems offer even more space for lower prices.

MODEM   A modem is the piece of hardware that allows your computer to connect to the Internet through the phone lines. Besides connecting you to the Web, a modem can also be used for faxing and file transfer, and, with the right software, as a telephone answering device. Modems are rated by the speed at which they can process bits of information over the phone lines, known as the

BAUD rate or bits per second (BPS). Most modems on the market today can operate at 28,000 to 58,000 BPS.

Modems used to be external equipment, but today they are usually incorporated into your computer's hard drive.

OTHER COMPONENTS   Other components that you will need to enhance your Web experience are a sound card, a graphics or video card, a CD-ROM drive, and a 3.5-inch disk drive, which are usually standard equipment on most systems you can buy now. Things such as a CD-ROM drive are not necessary for connecting to the Web, but it's good to have when you're installing software, because most of it comes on CD-ROM today. A floppy disk drive is handy when downloading information off the Web and for saving backups of your files.

Connecting to the Web

As part of your startup package, your Internet provider will often give you a CD containing a selection of software for connecting to the Web (called a Web browser). If your provider doesn't offer this, then there are sites on the Internet where you can get the latest version of the various software programs. No matter which program you choose, the important thing is to become familiar and comfortable with its features and capabilities.

Selecting an Internet Service Provider (ISP)

When selecting your ISP, you want to find a company with an established reputation that offers high-quality services at reasonable prices. You can certainly consider some of the more well-known servers (like AOL); however, don't rule out local servers, which may be much less expensive. For example, Sirona pays $189 per year for her unlimited-access Internet connection plus 15 MG of Web site space.

Here are some questions to ask when interviewing potential Internet service providers:

- What is the annual fee, and what does it include? How much time do you get online per month or year? Does the price include Web site space? Do they offer a discounted price for a simple hookup?
- Do they have a tech-support line available for answering questions and helping with problems? Be sure the service number is either a local or toll-free number.
- What type of payment options are available? Not all companies require a credit card number.
- What speed modem can their system support? As of this writing, a minimum of 28,800 BPS is considered a good industry standard, but 56,000 BPS is widely available.
- What is the company's user-to-line ratio? It should be under ten for the best service. Otherwise every time you try to connect to the Internet, the line will be busy.
- What type of news feed do they have? A lot of information is available on the over 20,000 newsgroups online, and without a good feed it will be difficult to access many groups.
- Does the server have any restrictions about what you can put up on your Web site? If so, what are they?

Surfing the Internet

Kawabunga! Like a surfer who rides his board in the curl of an ocean wave, surfing the Net involves choosing a subject and following it to its conclusion, which on the Web means finding the information you need about such things as purchasing ritual tools, Celtic music, or like-minded people. The Internet offers information on just about any subject. The downside of this is that sometimes you become inundated with information, much of it not pertinent to your search. The next section gives you a brief overview about what the Internet

is about, how search engines work, and how to get the information and sites you want from your search efforts.

Search Engines

The number of Web pages on the Internet is astronomical, with the numbers increasing every day. Because of this volume there are Web databases known as search engines and directories. Each database carries anywhere from one to thirty million pages, which are indexed in different ways depending on the database. From this indexing, each Web database has a different search interface. These fall under three broad categories: (1) full text indexing, where every word is put in the database for searching (databases using this form of indexing include AltaVista and Open Text); (2) keyword indexing, where important words and phrases are used in the search (Lycos and Excite); and (3) human indexing, where someone looks over a site and decides where it belongs within a directory system (Yahoo and parts of Magellan).

You access the information in a Web database through one of two methods—a search engine or a directory, also known as a pick list. With a search engine you type in any terminology, and the engine searches the database, finding those Web pages that match the terms entered, and listing them by the degree of what the indexing program perceives relevant. Directories work like the yellow pages of a phone book; they list sites in categories, sub-categories, and so forth. In this way, you can start out with a broad category such as *pagan* and keep narrowing down your search to find what you need. The downside of directories is because they are indexed by humans, they contain fewer pages and the pages in the database are subject to human interpretation. Because of this, a directory structure is usually a good starting point for a search, after which you can surf off into a search engine.

The beauty of search engines is that they allow you to tie concepts together. When typing in keywords for a search, the idea is to use phrases and string ideas together in a simple and specific manner so the computer program understands what you want. Surfing can become frustrating because the results of your search can sometimes lead you on a proverbial wild-goose chase. One of ways to avoid this is to use synonyms in your search. If you are looking for ritual tools and your search results in sites for companies that manufacture wrenches, then you need to add other words to your query. It's good to avoid homonyms, or if you use them, then specify what you do and don't want. (If you're looking for Polish pagan rituals, you might want to tell the program to exclude listings for shoes—as in shoe *polish*.)

Returning to the example of searching for ritual tools, try synonyms such as *ritual items* or possibly adding the words *athame*, *chalice*, and *wand*. Once you type in one query, check out what the results are, and home in on what works and eliminate what doesn't. The more specific you are, the better your search results will be.

In some search engines such as Excite, you can query using Boolean logic, meaning they use the words *and*, *or*, and *not*, as a means of adding and excluding to your query. Pseudo-Boolean logic reduces the *and* to a + symbol and the *not* to a – symbol. For example, if you were looking for a book on Celtic rituals you might type your query in this way: "books and rituals and Celtic," indicating you only want books meeting all three criteria. If you were looking for books on either Celtic or Egyptian rituals, you might present it this way: "books and rituals and Celtic or Egyptian," meaning you are looking for either. The *not* is used to exclude certain elements in your search, and is always used with parenthesis. If you were looking for a book on Celtic and Egyptian rituals but you didn't want any books on Scottish rituals, you would type, "books and rituals and Egyptian or Celtic not Scottish." The best way to search is to start out with an abstract or large term and then narrow it down into specifics: rituals, then Celtic or Egyptian, then Beltane, for example.

While computers are very orderly in the way they work, search engines are not. Most people are disappointed at first with search results because they don't often immediately yield the desired information. It takes a bit of hunting and detective work to get good results. Why? Because there is so much information on the Internet that it's like walking into five thousand libraries at once, with the books on the shelves all mixed up! So, don't expect that this library will yield orderly results. However, with time and practice you'll find you get better at surfing. Some hints that work include:

- Break your search down to the lowest common denominator. For example, if you're doing a search about native trees and flowers, you might think the best way to search would be by using tree+ flower, but actually a better choice is plants.
- Add no more than one or two words to the denominator at the outset of your search. Too many words yield results that will make no sense.
- Use the services provided by search engines themselves. For example, when looking for sacred sites in a particular state or country, go to Yahoo's travel links. Look up that state or country and its associated links. Many of the sites provided then have internal search engines that will hunt for what you want to find!

A couple of the places Sirona likes to begin when surfing the Net are www.37.com and www.happytrails.com. Both of these contain listings for multiple search engines. One of the search engines that Sirona likes beyond Yahoo, Excite, Lycos, Hotbot, and AltaVista is www.beaucoup.com, a directory-style engine that contains a wealth of information and sites. Another engine, www.dogpile.com, is an engine that takes your query through a variety of other engines, which it lists as it searches through them. We have not had a chance to check them all out, so if you find a really great search engine, e-mail us at www.dcsi.net/~bluesky or www.loresinger.com and let us know about it.

Yellow Pages, People Search, City Maps

These services, offered by several search engines, are particularly useful for Wiccans. Have you ever gone to a gathering, gotten the address for a new tribe member or a terrific merchant, and then promptly lost it on the way home? Yellow pages and people searches help us reestablish those important webs in our lives.

Light's On, Nobody's Home

On occasion, you may click on a search result and suddenly find there's no DNS entry or you get a response saying "we've moved!" Now what? First case, review your search results again (if necessary, go through a couple of pages of them). Frequently the Web page you wanted will have another listing that connects properly.

E-Mail

Considering the ever-rising cost of postage these days, e-mail is a God(dess)send for many people. It not only allows you to send a message for the cost of a local phone call, but the message arrives quickly, often within minutes or hours of sending it.

Most ISPs provide free e-mail software, such as Eudora Lite, when you sign up for their service. Both of the major browsers (Internet

Explorer and Netscape) include e-mail software as well. Also, many search engines offer free e-mail addresses just for registering with their site. Registering usually involves filling out an online form. One of the downsides of e-mail is what is known as spam—junk e-mail. If you find you are the victim of spam mail and would like it to stop, first contact the party sending the unwanted e-mail and tell them to take you off their mailing list. If they persist in sending you e-mail after notifying them then reply saying that you will report them to their provider. If they continue, contact their provider and tell them the problem. The provider is the part of the e-mail address that comes after the @ sign. Contacting the provider will almost always solve the problem.

Safety Measures

There some inherent downsides to surfing the Internet, but these can be avoided pretty well by taking some simple precautions. This section will give you helps and hints to safeguarding yourself and your computer from Internet abuses.

Utility Programs

Norton Utilities is a fantastic solution to a lot of minor problems that come up with computer hardware and software. Hardware that's getting cluttered, overwriting the wrong things, or that's experiencing odd glitches can often be diagnosed using this program. If the problem is fixable, it will ask you if you want the repair made. Norton also helps defragment your hard drive, clean up duplicate files, and keep everything orderly inside the system's virtual filing cabinet.

Norton offers other assistance for software errors, like file recovery or reconstruction. You won't always get the whole file back if it was wiped out by a computer error, but at least this offers a chance of partly recouping your loss. Norton also has formatting options for disks, and disk checks to make sure your older software is still working its best. If not, Norton can clean up parts of the disk that have the potential for experiencing reading errors.

Virus Protection

We highly recommend an automatic virus scan that checks your hard drive each time you boot up. You will need to regularly download updates to this program (most companies that offer virus-protection software also have Web sites for getting updates) since new viruses are introduced daily.

How to Avoid Sticky Cyber Situations

It is very important that people realize that the Internet is the perfect hiding ground for con artists and other individuals with bad intentions. Remember, anyone can set up a Web site that looks like it's a "real" company, and anyone can present himself or herself falsely over the Internet. Even the most savvy computer person can be fooled by flashy presentations. Consequently, it's prudent to take some precautions to stay out of harm's way.

If ordering anything online, try to get some referrals or references from the company first. Check any addresses or phone numbers for the company in a yellow-pages search engine to make sure it's not a front. Keep hard copies of all transactions between the company and yourself so that if any difficulties result you can report them to their server and the Better Business Bureau. Note that while some companies offer secure servers for credit card transactions, this has only recently become more available. However, most credit card companies will investigate potential fraud and even credit your account when such a situation arises.

When looking for services online, don't accept just any claim or endorsement. Follow them up as you might when looking for a personal physician. Or, go to services that are recommended by people you know personally. Yes, this can take a little extra time or limit your choices a bit, but you'll be much happier in the long run.

How to Report Internet Misconduct

You do not have to simply roll over and accept Internet misconduct. In fact, there's quite a bit you can do when an individual or a company is misusing the Internet.

- Keep excellent records of the abuse on your computer and on paper. Without these records you have no proof of the problem.
- Network with everyone you know, let them know about your problem, and ask them to spread the word. Let the Internet work for you to warn others of the situation. This networking process should include any related newsgroups or bulletin boards you can find. By making posts in these places, you increase the number of people you can warn.
- E-mail the offender's ISP using the subject line "abuse." These reports go to a special department for review, and may result in the denial of service to the offender.
- Report abuse by a business to the Better Business Bureau. Use the search-engine yellow pages to help locate the right place to send information.

Setting Up Your Computer Altar

The word *altar* means "a high place." This height, however, is not achieved so much by altitude as by attitude. An altar represents something greater than yourself. It is a spiritual doorway through which we commune with spirits and the divine. So long as you approach it with the proper respect and a little creativity, any place in your home can become a mini altar, including your computer space.

Now, it probably seems a bit odd to think about a surface cluttered with papers, disks, pencils, CDs, and computer parts as holy, but if you're going to work magic here, the first step is to change your outlook. The modern Wiccan is inventive and practical, considering everything in and around the sacred space of home for its inherent magical potential. In this case, you'll be focusing in on your computer and the surrounding area.

While the way each person creates an altar is highly personal, here are some general guidelines to help you get started.

Observation, Reflection, and Gathering

Look at the amount of space you're dealing with, where the computer
is set up (in terms of north, south, east, or west), and where you
could possibly place some elemental and God/dess representations.

Next think about what things, to you, represent each element that
will also be useful as you use the computer. You probably won't have
a lot of space available, so you'll want to make thoughtful choices. For
example, Trish uses a desk lamp anointed with oil to represent the fire
element (or sometimes the presence of spirit), which she also uses to
see better; a large goblet to represent water, which holds her pens
and pencils; a quartz crystal for earth (and energy), which she can use
as a paperweight; and an electric fan or the computer speakers for air!
All of these things, except the crystal, were already on her desk. She
just thinks of them differently now. Sirona uses a large cedar trunk
covered by a red cloth with Celtic knotwork on it as her computer
altar. She has a large clear crystal point, a one-inch amethyst sphere,

a malachite pyramid, and an oak ball (all representing earth) next to her monitor. On the left side of the monitor is a small earth-colored bowl representing earth, which holds paperclips. A stoneware cup representing water holds power-animal pens, pencils, a small ruler (all earth symbols), and a brass letter opener (fire). The desk lamp (fire) is decorated with the figurine of a stag, draped in stars (spirit), and anointed with essential oils (air). A green star sticker on the left side of her computer screen is for the Goddess, with a red sticker on the right side of her screen for the God. A miniature besom sits against the left side of her computer tower.

Some other examples include: a jar filled with coins to represent earth; an aromatic candle for air, spirit, or fire; blue pens for water (change the color to change the element); a red mouse pad for fire (again, you can change the color to reflect your intention or a different correspondence); a bowl for earth (which you can use to hold your offerings—or munchies, depending on the day), and so forth. The possibilities are as endless as your imagination. More ideas along these lines will be explored later in this chapter.

When choosing your elemental representations, remember to consider any others who share your living space (like children or pets). "Safety first" is an important element of Web Witching. You'll want to specifically avoid any toxic substances, liquids that will stand for any period of time, tiny things that children could swallow, or extremely fragile things, parts of which could end up in your keyboard, printer, or disk drives.

Gather together all of the items you have designated for symbolic purposes. Smudge them with some sage, cedar, or sweetgrass, or pass them through sandalwood incense smoke to cleanse any residual energies that may not be positive. If the item isn't sensitive to water, dip it in a mixture of lemon juice and water or sea-salt (if possible) water for similar effects.

This cleansing step is especially important if the chosen objects have been near your computer for some time. It's normal to become frustrated, yell, or swear at your machine when it isn't cooperating as you'd like it to. This leftover negativity is something you defi-

nitely don't need to add to the magical equation! It is just as important to cleanse your objects if others have handled them a lot, as
you don't necessarily want all that random energy influencing your
magic. It's best to clear it out and start with a clean slate.

Consecrating, Blessing, and Energizing

These tokens are about to take on a very important role as part
of your altar. Take the time to properly consecrate your computer altar
items by blessing and energizing them. As you do this, the objects
cease to be mundane objects; they become sacred tools. Blessing is
something that can be done in any way suited to your path. Many
people simply put their hands palms-down over the objects and pray
to and merge with their God/dess to sanctify the token for its purpose.
You can also merge with the elemental energies the item symbolizes. If
you're not accustommed to praying or can't think of any good words,
use the Charge of the Cyber Goddess or God provided in chapter 5.

Energizing doesn't require a lot of intricacy either, just some seri-
ous concentration and merging. Think of energizing like plugging in
to the electrical current of the universe. The purpose of this is to
charge up the chosen token's power. Some people accomplish this
by putting the object in sunlight, moonlight, or both, or in water or
burying it in the earth for a period of time. Other people carry the
object for several weeks so it gets saturated with their personal
energy. Still others meditate with the tool or token, directing energy
into it. All of these approaches hold merit. Use the one that makes
the most sense to you, considering your personal tradition, the ulti-
mate purpose of the object, and its essential qualities. For example,
something intended to represent fire is best charged in sunlight,
while a water or moon token is best charged in moonlight.

Placement

After following all of the previous steps, you can now put these consecrated items around your work area. If possible, the elemental

symbols should go near their coinciding compass point on your desk. This may differ depending upon your tradition. Sirona uses north for earth, east for air, south for fire, west for water, and center for spirit. Don't go crazy rearranging things; just be mindful of where you place each object. As you set the token down, you might want to give it an activating phrase like those used in invocations. This will allow you to turn its spiritual energy on and off as needed. Whisper the phrase to the object three times to activate it and a fourth time to turn it off. For example:

Turn on your elemental charm,
Protect me from any harm.

or

Switch on and thrive,
Breathe the elements alive.

Even when these objects are inactive they will still remind you of divine powers and your magic. This is very important in a world where busy schedules allow only a little time for the sacred. The more often we think of those powers and find ways to bring them into daily life, the better it is for our spirit, magic, and world.

Computer Altar Components and Focals

Sometimes it can prove difficult coming up with a functional design for your computer altar without a lot of fuss. This section will give you some starting ideas to help that process along. Mind you, this is only the tip of the figurative iceberg. Please add healthy portions of personal vision and intuition when creating your computer altar. Applying these two factors will determine how satisfying the end result will be for you. (Note: elemental correspondences for everyday objects and computer components follow later in this chapter.)

Aromatics

Included in this category we find smudge, incense, essential oils, flowers, potpourri, perfumes, cologne, and air fresheners. For thousands of years aromatics appeared on altars as offerings to the gods and goddesses, were burned in temples to purify the worshipers, and also represented the prayers of the faithful. With this in mind, using aromatics at your computer altar is quite fitting.

Aromatics fill the air around you with harmonious magical vibrations. They can also double as aromatherapy, too! You can choose four different aromas to represent the elements. Diffusers and air fresheners are good for the air element, while incense, when it is burning, also represents fire as well as air (smoke). Ah, but we're not done yet!

Dab your computer screen with insightful oils to help with Web Witching (sandalwood or lavender are good choices). Do not use oils on radiation shields such as NoRad, but instead dab a drop or two by the fan holes on the sides and top of your computer monitor. (Be careful not to get any of the oil in the holes!) You can also put a drop of essential oil on a desk lamp to slowly release its energy into the room. Dab yourself with your favorite scents to mark your space and keep your area clear of unwanted energies and guests while you are working magic. The possibilities are nearly endless!

Art

Depending on where your computer is situated and how much space is surrounding it, paintings, posters, statuary, and other artistic touches can really make a difference to the overall ambiance of your computer altar. For example, Trish keeps a framed Celtic greeting card on the wall behind her desk that depicts the God and Goddess from the grail mythos. She also has a painting of a fairy rising toward the sky, symbolizing the soul's quest, creativity, and the power of faith in helping us rise above circumstances. Sirona has a framed anniversary card of the Goddess in the forest, a picture of an

English castle next to her computer tower, and a print of *The Accolade* by Edmund Blair Leighton. A clear quartz crystal and a small stained-glass disk with three roses and a butterfly hang above her desk, representing transformation and transcendence. Thanks to the large market for New Age items, there are quite a few choices open to the Web Witch: get a carving of your totem animal, find a meditative poster, put a symbolic light catcher on a nearby lamp, or whatever. What's most important is that the art reflects your spiritual path and the sacred energy you're creating around your computer altar.

Candles

Candles are among the nearly indispensable tools of the Craft. We use them to focus our attention, for spells, rituals, and divination, as well as shamanic journeys and wish magic. The only downside to using candles as part of your computer altar is the safety risk. Use enclosed candles (like those at the supermarket that come in glass containers) or hurricane lamps. They're less likely to cause a fire or spill wax on your system. Small votives or tealights in deep glass holders also work well.

Candles can represent the presence of spirit on your altar, an element (by its color), a personal goal (by color, aroma, or carving), so they're very flexible. If your space isn't suited to candles, use a small penlight or flashlight instead during rituals. Try using a small lamp for illuminating your altar. (Even a portable book lamp will work well.) You can change the color of the lamp bulb to match the desired symbolism. If you use a light box underneath a large crystal, you can use different colored crystals or thin glass plates or plastic films to create the color harmonic you desire.

Colors

We know from psychological studies that color acts on the conscious and subconscious mind in potent ways. This is also what makes color correspondences so helpful to Web Witching. Better still, very few people visiting your home will think twice about a prominent color scheme (it won't scream "witch!" if you have magic-anxious friends or family members).

In choosing colors for your computer altar bear in mind that the color of *any* object on your altar can be symbolic as long as you treat it reverently. For example, if you're lacking space on your desk and want to add a functional earth color, how about a black or brown typing stand? If that takes up too much space, consider a black stapler or even green-tinted paper clips (these can be purchased at an office supply store). Here's a brief list of color correspondences for your reference:

BLACK   Banishing, rest, grounding, protection, unknown potential, ether, also represents all elements. Use when your computer's power is off.

BLUE   Harmony, clarity, happiness, peace, water. A good choice for background color on your computer screen and pictures around your computer area.

BROWN   Grounding, nurturing, stability, earth. Keep this color under your power source to discourage surges and to encourage prosperity.

GOLD   Higher wisdom, wealth, strength, symbolizes the sun, fire/air. Use this color to promote learning, magical power, and wealth.

GRAY   Mastery, mystery, wisdom, symbolizes the great potential of spirit or oneness, water, or air. Computer disks are most often gray or black. Use sparingly to designate areas of skill.

GREEN   Nature, growth, healing, earth, or water. A great color to keep your computer running smoothly and your database growing.

ORANGE   Friendship, happiness, productivity, fire, or earth. A good color for your tower (or wherever you house your hard drive). Or place an orange cloth under your tower for healing and protection and to avoid crashes.

PINK   Kinship, gentle love, fire, or water. Keep this color near your modem to improve goodwill for Web Witching.

PURPLE   Spiritual matters, magical ability, power, leadership, water, or air. Keep some purple highlights near your computer screen since this is where the "windows of your soul" (your eyes) will be searching for information.

RED   Passion, energy, determination, power, fire. Another good color for your computer's power source, but keep it an even-toned red to avoid too much energy. Red stickers can also be used. A red altar cloth works well as the base for your computer altar and keeps you motivated while you are working.

SILVER   The moon, emotion, renewal, magic, water. A silver lamp, pentacle, or small goddess statue make excellent additions to your cyber space.

WHITE   Protection, purity, spirit. An excellent color for software housing (or disks) since these are among the most sensitive parts of your system.

YELLOW   Creativity, communication, air. Keep this color near your keyboard. Yellow-gold citrine is a perfect stone to have handy in your cyber space as it activates and balances mental activity.

Computer Wand

Some computers come with these attached (small styli that are used to touch the screen to give commands). Alternatively, you can consider your mouse to be a wand, since it "points" the way to power.

Crystals, Stones, Metals, and Minerals

What's a good witch to do without a few good rocks? Most Wiccans are drawn to all kinds of stones and minerals because they reconnect us with the Earth Mother in a highly tactile and visual way. In esoteric traditions, stones represent the bones of the Goddess in the form of the earth.

Also, for thousands of years shamans have used crystals in healing and spirit journeying, and people offered gems and minerals as
gifts to the goddesses and gods, used them in spells, and generally
regarded stones as having inherent mystical energies that could be
tapped and utilized. The use of crystals and minerals is well worth
considering for your computer altar since a few stones won't take up
much space. Just be sure to keep your stones a safe distance (at least
one foot) from your hard drive and disks because they have been
known to hold a magnetic charge and could play havoc with your
system.

One way to integrate stones into your cyber space is to set up
Cyber Space Markers. Take four crystals or stones that correspond to
the four elements plus one representing spirit (a spherical or egg-
shaped crystal is perfect) and put them on your desk at the four
directional points. Place the spirit crystal in the center. Sirona uses
fine-pointed clear quartz crystals to mark the four corners of her
sacred cyber space. She uses a one-inch amethyst ball to represent
spirit, and often uses the ball to exercise her fingers and hands while
working on the computer.

Before you set up your Cyber Space Markers, merge with the
crystals and imbue them with the energy of their respective quarters.
Keep these crystals in place around your cyber space and allow them
to become attuned to your cyber space. You can use breathing techniques, music, drumming, chanting, color, scent, and textures to
amplify the energy and effect of your Cyber Space Markers. For
example, you can increase the energy of your Markers by simply
placing a cloth of the corresponding color underneath each of the
stones.

If space won't allow for you to use Cyber Space Markers, tuck
your stones into a pouch, mojo, or medicine bag, and hang them off
the computer screen or typing stand instead (again, a safe distance
away from your hard drive and disks). Other suggestions are to sus-
pend your stones in a bag from your desk lamp or hang a crystal
ball above your work space to keep the chi circulating. If push
comes to shove, you can always carry small stones in your pocket,

making yourself the bearer of the sacred space as you approach your work area! Of all your choices for Web Witching, clear quartz is perhaps the most universally useful stone. It can hold any type of energy you chose to put in it, and since quartz is often used in technology as an energy conduit, it fits in with the techno-magic theme. Better still, quartz points aren't overly expensive and can be used as an alternative wand or symbol of the God (round stones represent the Goddess). Another good choice to keep handy is fluorite to stimulate the conscious mind. While Web Witching is a function of the super-conscious, you still need your logic and reasoning in order to run your system efficiently. For balance, use an amethyst or lapis to emphasize the psychic and spiritual aspects of your work.

Beyond this, the choice of what stones, metals, and so on you keep on your computer altar is purely personal, and there are a lot of options! Just remember that a stone need not be a permanent altar fixture. You can add one suited to the magic you're doing at the moment, then tuck it away for another day. For example, on a day when you're focusing on networking, bring a carnelian. During a session when you're using your computer for divination, bring a moonstone.

Warning: Do not use lodestone or other stones of a magnetic nature around your hard drive or disks. The magnetism can wipe out data or cause other glitches just by being close to the hard drive or disks.

Following is a list of stones and some key energetic qualities and magical applications for your easy reference.

Agate   grounding, building patterns, self-confidence
Amazonite   creativity, prosperity, receiving energy and messages
Amethyst   divine connection, mental clarity, healing, astral
    projection
Aquamarine   inspiration, altered states of consciousness, sharpen-
    ing intuition
Aventurine   healing, Internet adventures, imagination

Bloodstone   creativity, higher knowledge, healing

Calcite   memory enhancement, learning, astral projection

Carnelian   sun and fire, mental focus, sex magic

Citrine   mental quickness, clarity, manifestation

Clear quartz   healing, divine communication, shamanism, all
    kinds of magic

Fluorite   harmony, spiritual awakening, stimulating the conscious
    mind, astral projection

Hematite   grounding, manifesting, protection

Jade   love, protection, earth, meditation

Lapis lazuli   shape-shifting, all types of magic, lucid dreaming,
    divination

Malachite   visions, moving energy, prosperity, rapport with nature
    and deity; also neutralizes the radioactivity of the computer
    screen and tower

Moldavite   stimulates intuition, accelerates learning, shape-shifting

Moonstone   divination, healing, enhances artistic abilities, moon
    magic

Rose quartz   divine love, spiritual awakening, friendship, fertility

Smoky quartz   neutralizes radioactivity of computer screen and
    tower, grounding, healing, divination.

Sodalite   vision, neutralizes radiation, mental clarity, healing

Tiger's eye, cat's eye   mental concentration, merging, invisibility,
    protection, shape-shifting

Turquoise   ritual, astral projection, rapport with elementals, healing

Music

Music is the universal language and it is among one of the most
magical mediums in the world. The ancient bards used words and
music to weave power into an entertaining tapestry for listeners.
Buddhist monks use mantras, shamans sing their magic, and Wiccans often chant. So having a little music playing to improve your
focus for Web Witching isn't a bad idea, and it's certainly a better
option than leaving the TV on.

Check through samplers of New Age artists (some Web sites offer sound files you can listen to) and find those that create the right atmosphere for your Web Witching. Some personal favorites of both Trish and Sirona include Loreena McKennitt, David Arkenstone, Enya, Aine Minogue, Maireid Sullivan, and Mickey Hart, as well as Ottmar Liebert, Oasis, Alan Stivell, Kula Shaker, and Kitaro. Note that if you have a CD-rom drive, it can play audio CDs. Some newer systems include radio tuners, and there are plenty of Internet radio stations you can listen to by using your Web browser.

Place Mats and Altar Cloths

This category includes coasters and your mouse pad. Choose these so their color or patterns reflect the magic you're creating. Or, perhaps consider changing them seasonally. An enormous assortment of mouse pads are available to suit even the most finicky pagan! Also, there's a practical purpose for mats and cloths. If you accidentally spill something, they will absorb some of the liquid, thereby decreasing the chance of damage to your system. As a general rule keep beverages, liquids, and water-filled vases away from your entire computer system. Place these things on an adjacent surface such as a small table or stool, where they will do the least amount of harm if tipped over.

Yourself

It is amazing how many people forget that the body is a portable altar and is a sacred space too. Some people have favorite sweats or a Craft robe they like to wear when surfing the Wiccan Web. But even when you have no components or adornments, you have the essentials of magic with you at all times: able hands, a loving heart, and a focused will. With this in mind, your cupped hand becomes a symbol of the water element, your pointed finger becomes an athame or wand, your feet touch the earth and ground you, and your head reaches toward the sky and air. Don't feel limited by the lack of trinkets and toys; they're fun, but they're only tools to help increase your focus. Web Witching begins inside you, and as long as

you remember that, you'll need little else other than your computer
and your imagination to begin.

The Magic of Everyday Items

Earlier in this chapter we talked briefly about using the elemental
correspondences of everyday items as a space-saving technique for
your computer altar. In order for this idea to work for you, you'll
first have to stop thinking of things as just having a tangible presence. Anything that exists in this world also bears some type of
astral presence or energy pattern that can be used in magic, if we
recognize and empower that presence or pattern.

Here is a list of items often found in an office or computer room
with elemental correspondences and magical associations for your
consideration:

ITEM	ELEMENT	ASSOCIATIONS/APPLICATIONS
Calculator	Earth/fire	Combining elements, patterning
Calendar	Earth	Cycles, planning, socialization
Cup	Water	Alertness, conscious mind, chalice
Glass	Water	Cleansing, body connection, chalice
Glue	Earth/water	Binding, strong attachment
Letter opener	Fire	Opening up possibilities, athame
Paper	Earth/air	Protection, knowledge, communication
Paper clip	Earth/fire	Connection, loose security
Pencil/pen	Air/earth	Communication, alternative wand
Rubber band	Earth	Flexible connection, cosmic metaphor
Ruler	Air/earth	Evaluation, details, God image
Scissors	Fire	Separation, alternative athame
Snack bowl	Earth	Sustenance, Goddess image
Stamps	Water/air	Movement, messages
Stapler	Earth/fire	Binding, penetrating attachment
Tape	Earth	Binding, connection, protection
Telephone	Air	Connection, information, networks

Your Computer's Elemental Correspondences

As with the items around your computer, each part of the system has elemental correspondences that you may wish to use in your Web Witching. Since this idea is broaching on "cutting edge" magic, what we're giving here are personal, instinctual associations. In discussing this section, we considered what each part of the computer does, and to which elemental correspondence that function best related. Be that as it may, you may feel differently about these parts, and you should always trust those instincts over anything found in a book.

ITEM	ELEMENT	ASSOCIATIONS/APPLICATIONS
Computer user	Spirit	Conduit of divine energy/oneness
Disk	Earth	Preservation, protection, knowledge
Drives	Air/fire	Energy, motivation, movement
Hard drive	Earth	Storing power/information
Keyboard	Water	Creative flow, communication
Mouse	Air	Directional focus, alternative wand
Mouse pad	Earth	Rest, grounding ideas
On switch	Fire	Active energy, stimulation
Printer	Air	Manifestation
Radiation screen	Earth	Protection, cleansing
Scanner	Fire	Seeing the truth, visual perspective
Screen	Fire	Visualization, imagination
Surge protector	Water	Controlling diverse energies

Screen Savers

Screen savers are programs that were originally designed to save wear and tear on monochrome computer monitors; they are designed to come on after no keyboard strokes or mouse clicks have registered for a set period of time. These days, screen savers are intended more for visual appeal and are used as a source of personal expression.

For Wiccans, the visual element of screen savers can be particularly useful. Computers that use the Microsoft Windows platform often have a choice of screen savers, one of which is called the Scrolling Marquee. It consists of a blank screen with words or phrases scrolling across it. Users of Windows 95, 98, and 2000 can find this option in their Control Panel under Display.

The Scrolling Marquee screen saver has the advantage of allowing you to type in anything you want, such as spells, rituals, dedications, and affirmations, and these words will scroll across your screen in large, colorful letters every time the screen saver comes on. It provides the perfect channel for learning spells and chants easily as you work near your computer. For example, you could type in a simple blessing spell, such as "Goddess of love, God of wealth, gift me with happiness and good health! Ayea, Ayea Kerridwen! Ayea, Ayea Kernunnos! So be it."

Sirona likes to change her Scrolling Marquee screen savers regularly depending on her needs, moods, and the seasons. Her latest Scrolling Marquee says, "Spring is everywhere, in the flowers, in the air! It's a Great Day to be alive, here and now. Ayea Hertha, Ayea Belenus, Ayea All!" Remember to be creative and have fun.

You can also download screen savers off the Internet. We searched for pagan screen savers, and many sites came up, including this one: www.pagans.org/~firerose/pagan1.htm. Some sites offer free screen savers; others offer general and custom screen savers for a fee. If you have an idea of what you want, chances you can find a site on the Internet to satiate your screen saver desires. If not, there are also sites that can give you the code in Visual Basic for creating and programming your own screen savers. Screen savers that you download off the Internet or create yourself need to have the extension .scr and have to be loaded into your Windows directory.

In addition to screen savers, you can also choose the pictures that display when your computer first boots up, as well as the background picture on your computer screen. If you have a scanner, you can scan and use favorite pictures to personalize your computer desktop. Last Yule, Sirona loaded a photo of her family taken at Yule festivities the previous year, which then came up each time she turned on her computer. Again, like screen savers, seeing personal and meaningful images on your computer can have a constantly uplifting and empowering effect on your sense of well-being as well as on all of your magic.

Consecrating Your Computer Altar

Once everything is in place and you feel comfortable with your altar's configuration, the next step is consecration. While this might seem like a formidable task to those not accustomed to being their own priests or priestesses, relax. To consecrate something simply means to set it aside and dedicate it to some sacred power or purpose. This can be accomplished through prayer, by a vocal declaration to the four directions, or by other methods that seem fitting to your magical tradition. Keep the time of day, season, and astrological influences in mind when consecrating your altar items.

For readers who would like a construct to follow, here's one example:

CYBER CONSECRATION RITE

Stand in front of your computer altar. Take a deep cleansing breath and focus on your intentions. Think of all the ways in which you plan to use this area for Web Witching. When you feel centered and in the right frame of mind for making a magical declaration, turn to the east and say:

Eastern Winds, carry my voice to the four corners of creation and witness this rite. Today I declare this area a sacred space—one in which my mind and spirit will find enrichment. Bless this spot with a breezy kiss of motivation and the power of communication.

Turn to the south (clockwise) and say:

> *Southern Fires, spark upon hearing my words and witness this rite.*
> *Today I declare this area a sacred space—one in which my body and*
> *spirit will be energized and purified. Bless this spot with a warm kiss*
> *of power, and the energy of God.*

Turn to the west (continuing clockwise) and say:

> *Western Waters, crest upon hearing my words and witness this rite.*
> *Today I declare this area a sacred space, one in which my body,*
> *mind, and spirit will find wholeness and inspiration. Bless this spot*
> *with a wave of creativity and the powers of the Goddess.*

Turn to the north and say:

> *Northern Soil, wake upon hearing my words and witness this rite.*
> *Today I declare this area a sacred space, one in which my mind and*
> *spirit will find firm foundations. Bless this spot with the loam of*
> *growth and the power of maturity. So mote it be.*

If you wish, it is appropriate at this point to move to the center of
the circle, or if you prefer, just in front of the altar again and welcome or pray to Spirit (Goddess or God) for its blessing.

Maintaining and Augmenting Cyber Sacred Space

Since many Wiccans and pagans today live in urban environments
that slowly siphon off positive magical energy, its very important
that you have some type of regular maintenance schedule for your
computer altar. You'll rarely see a cluttered, dusty temple because
messiness is equated with negative or unproductive energy. Similarly, for the Web Witch, the computer area is an electronic temple
and it needs to be kept clean both physically and spiritually. As you
probably already know, computers and dust are not compatible.

   A monthly effort is usually effective for maintaining energy levels.
During this time you should move everything on your computer
altar, dust the surface, clean your elemental tokens, reorganize, and

then "reset" the energy. Make your computer altar a suitable home for the sacred powers it represents! When you clean your cyber space, use your imagination and create a ritual out of the experience. For example, Sirona uses a small besom to remove dust between keys on her keyboard, while chanting a simple clearing spell, "Dust be gone, sweep it clean. Bless the Mother, keep her green."

Throughout the process you may choose to assemble things in your cyber space differently; you may want to take away some items or add others. This is perfectly natural; so follow your instincts and imagination. All that's happening is that you're expressing outwardly the spiritual changes that have taken place within, extending and evolving your magical awareness.

Now that you have your sacred cyber space set up and organized, the next step is to get down to magic making. The next chapter spells out the how-tos of computer magic. Web Witching is all about extending your magical skill using your computer as a sacred and powerful tool. In the next chapter, we show you how to surf the waves of cyberspace in ways that you have never dreamed of, with suggestions for magical focals and practical spellwork.

3

TECHNO-SPELLS

In this section we're going to discuss many ways to cast spells using your computer as either a focus or a tool for the magic. Some of these spells are intended to help keep your computer running at its best, like an antivirus spell that accompanies regular antivirus scans, while others smooth the way for effective Web Witching efforts. Before you begin, however, remember that it is important to approach magical activity in the best possible way. Follow these helpful hints to get started on the right foot.

- Make sure you're in the right mood for working magic. In other words, don't be angry, tired, or out of sorts. Not only will these kinds of physical and mental conditions bend your magical energy incorrectly, but it can also leach into your computer system and cause glitches.
- Whenever you're going to use your computer for a spiritual endeavor of any kind, approach it differently. Meditate, merge, or pray beforehand. Wash your hands to rinse away negativity (keep your keyboard clean too), and put worldly thoughts aside. Focus wholly on your intention.

- Try to ensure that you won't be interrupted during your spell, ritual, meditation, or whatever. Interruptions tend to bend or disperse the energy you're creating because they distract you from the goal at hand. If you do get interrupted, it's best to start again from scratch if possible, or to take a short moment to recenter yourself and renew your focus through breathing and mental effort.
- As with any magic, personalize the spells we've provided so that the words or components have meaning to you, and you're comfortable with the process. Use your intuition and be creative.
- Before you start anything, just sit in front of your system for a few moments. Are you comfortable? Is the desk well situated near some natural ambient light? This might sound trivial, but the energetic flow of your work area will make a big difference to the success rate of your magic.
- Create a sacred space through intention, will, word, and deed. If you set up your computer altar with objects that have an activating word, recite the word as part of creating the sacred space. A sample of a cyber-circle invocation is included in chapter 4.

Techno-Spell Components

Like any effective mystical recipe, techno-spells require the right balance of ingredients and combinations in order to manifest successfully. In keeping with the theme of this book, these ingredients can be those traditional to spellcraft or completely new components provided to us by the magic of technology. In either case, the purpose of this section is to provide you with a sample ingredient list to choose from to create your own cyber magic.

As you look over this list, you'll notice that some components serve as a focus, others become a prop, and still others support the magic symbolically. This diversity is very important for two reasons. First, each person's way of approaching magic reflects his or her path and vision. If you ask five people to choose the right focus, prop, or symbol for any theme, you're likely to get five different answers! So, any magical "cookbook" needs to offer variety as a spice.

Second, really good magic needs to have rich, sensual dimensions that, in turn, liberate your spiritual nature and give form to the magic in the real world. Having an assortment of components from which to choose allows the practitioner to build that sensual dimension in personally meaningful ways. Since there's no possible way we can include every potential cyber spell ingredient, we hope that you will add many more components to this list as your Web Witching abilities grow.

Traditional Components

In working spells that focus on your computer as a component itself, a medium for magic, or the intended recipient of the magic, the best place to begin is with tried-and-true, familiar parts. Innovation is wonderful, but tradition still deserves a place at your cyber altar. The following are just a few ways to integrate traditional spell components into your Web Witching efforts.

Candles

Candle magic is a must for all practicing Web Witches, and can be as simple as dedicating a candle to a special god or goddess by making a heartfelt dedication as you light the candle, or as elaborate as dressing the candle and creating grids with stones, herbs, and other items. Remember to keep candles a safe distance from your computer components because of wax spatters and the dangers of the candle being knocked over.

There is something inherently magical about a flickering candle flame, home to the elemental salamander. Candles speak a mystical language. The words are expressed by the dancing flame, the flow of smoke, and the popping and crackling of the burning wax. Candle chatter and the direction in which the flame moves all denote magical communication. In this way, each candle is unique and reflects its own personality when lit.

Different parts of the candle symbolize different things. The flame of the candle is the soul or spirit, and the wick is the vehicle of transmutation when lit. The halo of the flame symbolizes God/dess-hood, while the body of the candle is the physical world, and when lit, represents all of the elements. The candle smoke carries your intentions and deepest desires to the God and Goddess.

Candles come in all colors, shapes, and sizes. Match the color of your candle with your magical goal. (Please refer to the color meanings in the previous chapter.) To dress your candle for Web Witching, begin by washing it in cool sea-salt water and rinsing it in fresh water. Carve names, initials, and symbols three times on the candle body using a quill, pen, or athame. Next, apply essential oil (preferably consecrated) to the candle body, completely covering it. Place the candle on your computer altar in a fireproof container.

Build a power grid around your candle by surrounding it with a circle of nine (the number of the Goddess) crystals or gemstones such as clear quartz and citrine. Experiment with sacred geometric patterns of stones such as a pentacle, triangle, or zodiac circle and keep the directional corners of north, east, south, and west in mind. Try placing four stones that represent the four elements around your candle, or use talisman stones to impart magical qualities to your candle grid.

Next add selected herbs, sprinkling them inside the stone grid and on the candle itself. You can also carefully add herbs to the candle flame. Place other appropriate items around your candle or inside your stone circle such as flowers, shells, seeds, leaves, coins, and pentacles. Candles used in candle magic should be allowed to burn all the way down and go out naturally. If you do need to snuff out the candle, the best way to do so is by wetting your index finger and thumb and using them to extinguish the flame. Another option is using a consecrated candle snuffer, preferably a metal one. (Blowing a candle out blows out your magical energy.)

Sirona sets up a new candle magic grid and dresses, inscribes, and lights a special candle just before she starts each new book. She also created a Samhain desktop screen display using scanned photos of lit candles, which is yet another way to use candles when Web Witching. If you want to have a little techno-candle magic fun, use your scanner to place a virtual candle on your computer screen and build a virtual magical grid around it with other images you've scanned or downloaded from the Internet.

If you really don't like the idea of burning candles around your computer system, an alternative is to gather the pieces of candle wax that are left over from an appropriate candle magic spell or ritual and place them in a small pouch with a pinch of corresponding herbs. Keep this pouch on your computer altar.

An excellent mood-shifting tool, candlelight reflects off the computer's screen in marvelous ways. Try placing a candle in front of the screen and lighting it just before you begin a cyber spell. Use the flame as an initial focus to draw your eyes back toward the computer until the fire in both unite. Or, simply place a candle of a suitable color or shape near your system (in a fire-safe container, please) while you work your magic.

Flowers

Flowers also have metaphysical uses and qualities, and can be used to express feelings and magical intentions. For example, place a flower in a bud vase or glass and keep it on your computer altar a safe distance away from your computer components. Match the flower and its color with the magical spell. Following is a list of flowers and Web Witching uses:

African violet protection of system and cyber spellwork
Daffodil ease in logging on to the Internet, sun and spring cyber magic, brightening chat room sessions
Daisy used for keeping your system and spellcrafting fresh, for beginning Web projects
Dandelion granting wishes, calling in the cyber God/dess
Iris sacred to the cyber Goddess, longevity of hard drive, printer, scanner, and software
Jasmine sacred cyber love spells, cyber divination

Lily   protection while uploading and downloading to or from the
   Web or while trashing e-mail
Marigold   to induce prophetic and lucid cyber dreams, attract
   cyber faeries and spirits
Orchid   cyber inspiration, mastery, sacred cyber love, for a little
   cyber elegance during special chats or rituals
Rose   cyber love magic, divination, abundance, healing; excellent
   computer altar flower
Sunflower   inspiration, cyber sun magic, installing software
Tulip   cyber love magic, feminine symbol of expression

Herbs

Nature communicates her mysteries directly to us through color,
smell, taste, sound, shape, and texture as well as through more
subtle energies. Herbs are one of Nature's mysteries—simple yet
potent treasures for our use. The number of ways you can use herbs
in spells is nearly limitless. Trish, for example, uses bay leaves as
part of a spell for smooth computer operation (the leaves get left
under the base of the computer to keep the magic where it's most
needed). She also hangs a garlic bulb nearby whenever it seems like
there's a "ghost in the machine" as a way of banishing that persnickety energy. Sirona likes to crush fresh bay leaves in her hands
and then rub her hands over her keyboard to clear her mind just
before writing. For those readers who don't fancy themselves deco-
rating with herbs, you can burn them during a spell, use them in
potpourri as a kind of aromatherapy, or bundle them into computer
amulets and charms. You can also make small herbal sachets, which
are small pieces of natural cloth filled with herbs tied together. You
can hang these on your computer screen or on a desk lamp, where
the heat will enhance their aromatic qualities. Some common house-
hold herbs you might want to use in your cyber spells include:

Allspice berries   For a little extra luck with your system
Basil   Exorcising bad vibes and spirits from your machine

Catnip Attracts positive cyberspace energies and connections
Cayenne Increases your system's magical power
Echinacea Strengthens all cyber magic and cyber healing
Ginger For working on power-related system problems
Lemon rind Encourages a good rapport with your system
Lavender Promotes positive and peaceful Web Witching
Mint Heals hardware or software problems
Mustard seed Emphasizes the conscious mind
Nutmeg Keeps things running smoothly (a maintenance herb)
Rosemary Helps you remember important computer functions
Sage To extend the life of disks and drives

Incantations

The verbal element is an ancient and very valuable part of spell-craft. It charges the air around the practitioner with sympathetic vibrations for manifesting the spell's goals. The Druids felt that by knowing how to spell a word and speak it, a person had power over the object that word represented. The spoken word, like the written word, amplifies and directs magical power. What's really neat here for people whose computers are equipped with microphones or have software that allows the computer to read letters out loud is that you can record various incantations as sound files and play them back during spellcraft so that your computer joins your efforts! Note: this idea works with invocations, chanting, songs, and mantras, too.

Incense

Among the tools of many religious traditions we often find incense as a purifier, an offering, or as a representation of prayers rising to heaven. It also has the additional function of aromatherapy. (Note: For those who are bothered by incense smoke, there are smokeless incenses and essential oil diffusers.) What's nice about incense is that it is space efficient; most incense holders are small and fit nearly anywhere! Just be sure the ash doesn't get on your computer components. Around your sacred cyber space, incense helps clear the air of negative energy that not only adversely affect the magic but can cause static and disrupt smooth system operations. It also helps you move into an altered state of consciousness so important in magic. Some good choices for incense in your techno-magic space include:

Amber   Attracts goddess energies to your cyberspace
Carnation   For your system's health and longevity
Cedar   Purifies your cyberspace
Dragon's blood   A pinch increases the power of cyber magic
Frankincense   Use to consecrate your computer system
Honeysuckle   To emphasize the solar/logical nature when working
   on more concrete system problems
Jasmine   To emphasize a meditative and loving state of mind for
   Web Witching
Lilac   For synchronicity with your system
Myrrh   To break a hex or banish negative energy from the system
Sandalwood   For your system's health and spiritual focus
Sweetgrass   Attracts positive spirits to your cyber space
Vanilla   Attracts goddess energy and helps sweeten cyber spells
Violet   To protect your system and your sacred space

Music

Playing a special song or musical piece while Web Witching can help you to center and focus. Your body, mind, and spirit can learn to recognize a specific musical pattern and immediately associate it with magic, prompting an immediate shift in your awareness.

Most computers now come with a CD-rom drive, stereo speakers, and a microphone. This enables you to listen to tunes while you are surfing and Web Witching. Also, anyone who has a compatible sound card, such as SoundBlaster, has the ability to record and play back rituals, spells, chants, drumming, specific songs, and special effects. Be creative and be sure to add music whenever you connect to the Wiccan Web.

Oils

Essential oils are even more space efficient than incense. You can dab blessed, energized aromatic oils on your skin, clothes, sachets, computer altar, or computer screen! Dabbing oils on your keyboard, tower, or printer isn't a good idea because oils have a tendency to become tacky and gum up the works.

Remember—some oils may cause adverse allergic reactions when applied directly to your skin. If certain oils irritate your skin, an option is putting a couple of drops on a cotton ball and placing it on your computer altar or on top of your computer monitor by the air holes. Or you can burn aromatic oils in incense. If you're sensitive to smoke, you can use an aromatherapy diffuser or simply put a few drops in a small cup of boiling water and place the cup on or nearby your altar.

Anointing with oils has traditionally been used for consecrating altars and ritual tools and in spells for blessing, healing, empowering, and spiritual preparation. All of these functions are perfectly suited to cyber spells—blessing yourself or your system (rose is a good choice), healing your hard drive (try lotus or lavender), empowering your magic to reach its goal (vanilla), and preparing both yourself and your system for spiritual endeavors (sandalwood). Your sense of smell is the sense tied closest to memory and has a direct effect on your state of mind, so using a certain scent when Web Witching is just like playing a particular piece of music each time you do magic. The scent, like the piece of music, immediately triggers a magical response from you and sets the tone for the work, creating a certain "Web-scents-ability." Also, remember to use a drop of essential oil on paper and envelopes, and on every piece of correspondence that you send out, including your bills. This carries the magic into postal channels as well. Following is a list of Web Witching oils and some of their uses and properties. Select oils with scents that please and empower you.

Allspice   money spells, brings luck, cyber healing works
Almond   draws prosperity to you from the Web, connects you
   with your inner wisdom

Amber   for cyber rituals and spellwork, strengthens and soothes
the body, mind, and cyber spirit

Apricot   love magic, enhances creativity, great chat oil!

Balsam fir   mental clarity and precision, prosperity

Bay   enhances psychic abilities, divination, protection,
purification, healing, and attracts women on the Web

Benzoin   connects you with the cyber Goddess and God,
protection, calms and balances, prosperity spells—excellent
cyber ritual oil!

Carnation   consecrating computer altar items, protection, ancestor
magic, and finding lost relatives on the Internet

Cedar   cyber healing, purification, money spells, calms spiritual
energies, for cleansing your cyber sacred space

Chamomile   cyber love magic, prosperity spells, used for
relaxation

Cinnamon   enhances psychic powers, protection, chat stimulator

Citrus   mental focus and clarity, healing, beginning projects on
the Wiccan Web

Dragon's blood   protection, ridding yourself of negativity, cyber
love magic, directing magical energy on the Web

Ginger   strengthens magical power, healing, warms the spirit,
cyber love and sex magic

Hibiscus   enhances divination, cyber love and sex magic, for
accessing Web passions

Honeysuckle   protection, connects you with deity, strengthens
psychic and divination abilities, relaxation, cyber dream magic

Jasmine   love and dream magic, antidepressant, heightens
awareness

Lavender   purification, protection, creates an energetic balance
and harmony, excellent overall Web Witching oil

Mint   e-mail and messaging oil, protection, clarity, increases
memory and magical focus

Narcissus   enhances cyber divination, spiritual connection,
connects you with your inner voice

Patchouli   attracts surfers to your Web page, great for bringing
   more Web Witches to chat rooms, for attracting love and
   prosperity from the Internet

Pine   protection, strengthens magical focus and awareness,
   prosperity spells, and cyber rituals

Rose   for blessing yourself and your computer altar, brings luck
   and love, enhances cyber divination, balances magical energies.

Rosemary   increase memory and mental abilities, cyber love
   magic, purification, protection, and healing

Sage   protects your system from crashes and viruses, great to use
   when dumping your e-mail trash, balances magical energy,
   purification and for cleansing altar items and yourself

Sandalwood   for accessing the Goddess and God, protects you
   while Web Witching and surfing and during ritual and
   spellwork, harmonizes body, mind, and cyber spirit

Vanilla   cyber love magic, calms nerves, mental clarity, great chat
   room oil

Ylang-ylang   tension relief, love magic, strengthens your
   connection to deity and otherworlds of awareness, keeps you
   balanced during cyber ritual and spellwork

Stones

Stones, crystals, metals, and minerals collect and transmit magical energy as efficiently as your CPU. You can keep a few of these nearby to support a specific spell or to saturate your cyberspace with positive vibrations. You can use stone tinctures, those you make or the ones available from metaphysical and New Age stores, on computer altar items. Also wearing jewelry with stones imparts their qualities, especially if the setting allows the stone to touch your skin. Here's a list of some stones you might want to try:

Agate   grounding energies and solidifying spellwork

Amethyst   keeps your system running smoothly

Aventurine   good luck charm for successful Web Witching

Bloodstone   enhances your Web Witching creativity

Calcite   excellent Internet learning talisman

Carnelian   helps you properly express yourself over the Net, solar
cyber magic

Citrine   stimulates human-to-cyber communication

Clear quartz   for clarity in all computer projects

Clear quartz point   directs and projects energy over the Internet

Fluorite   accessing the conscious self and balance

Garnet   good luck for Internet businesses

Hematite   decreases and grounds out static

Jade   increases the longevity of your disks and drives

Lapis lazuli   enhances cyber psychic abilities and divination

Lava stone   protects your e-mail from flame wars

Malachite   for general supportive and protective power (and when
dealing with electrical problems)

Moldavite   aids in magical cyber quests and makes great corner
stones for your desk

Moonstone   balances electronic, cyber, and human emotions

Rose quartz   helps increase Web Witching self-esteem and
friendships

Serpentine   debugs your machine

Smokey quartz   grounds unwanted energies and absorbs harmful
radiation from computer components

Sodalite   excellent for cyber healing spells and to get Web
Witching energy flowing smoothly

Tiger's eye   enhances magical focus and cyber sight

Turquoise   prevents computer-related accidents (like coffee spills);
also for cyber psychonavigation and cyber star walking

Visual Devices

Visual focals such as photographs and tarot cards can be placed
on your computer altar to enhance your cyber spells. Also, magical
symbols can be integrated into your computer altar, either by plac-

ing them on tools and cards or by having the symbol in a file you can call up on your computer screen when appropriate.

Cyber Components

As we take our magic into the new millennium, we need to make an effort to get a little more creative with our vision and practices. Wicca has always been a growth-related belief system that adapts and changes with both the individual and the world. Cyber components give us yet another way of preparing for and living in a future where computers are going to become increasingly common and important to society.

Below you'll find a brief list of various computer parts and functions and their potential symbolism for spellcraft. As you read this, realize that the part need not be in functional order to work on a symbolic level. Indeed, since computer parts can be costly, you'll probably want to opt for used ones rather than new. On the other hand, there is some potency in the concept of "working" parts versus inactive or broken ones. So trust your instincts to know which is best considering the spell at hand.

CABLES   These represent networking, opening lines of communication, the flow of energy, and our connection to each other. Their pliable nature also makes them a good symbol of flexibility.

CDS   Because these are circular, they are a good symbol of the wheel of time and cycles. Trish charges her old ones with specific types of energy (accentuated by the CDs' color) and then uses them for coasters.

DISKS   Disks are a symbol of knowledge, and the ability to access that knowledge when it is most needed (or, for that matter, tuck it away). Because they are square, they can also represent the four quarters of creation.

FILE NAMES   When you're working on a specific type of long-term magic and you are keeping a record of this magic's progress in your computer, it helps to have creative names. For example, naming a directory or file LOVE, then opening that file, helps you "retrieve" that energy.

FONTS   The visual impression that your cyber spells make is very important, especially when you're sending the spell to someone else. Fonts can be used to make a file more attractive or set a specific mood. The only caution here is to make sure the recipient's system can open the associated file to accept the energy it contains.

GRAPHICS   Many computer programs have the ability to add graphics into any document. Even if the chosen imagery remains hidden, the energy imprint is there. Consider scanning in some magical sigils, runes, and symbols that you can combine with your spells and rituals for greater sensual dimension.

KEYBOARD   The keyboard represents messages, making a point, and manifestation (you think it, then you see it). Note that the specific keys carry meaning in themselves including the backspace or delete key for diminishing or banishing, the space key for designing visual sacred space on your screen, the shift key for shapeshifting work, and the equal key for matters of balance and symmetry. Also, the letters from a broken keyboard make a neat divination tool (information on this system will be covered in chapter 5).

MEMORY CHIPS   An excellent symbol of the conscious mind's ability to learn and remember.

MOUSE BALLS   An effective representation of the Earth, turning any situation around, movement, and cycles. An alternative "magic circle" (for this purpose, you can paint the ball with four elemental colors in the appropriate quarters).

SCREEN SAVERS   Overall, these represent carefully conserved and monitored energy. Whatever imagery you put here gets dispersed each time the screen saver comes into play.

SOUND CARDS Sound cards give external expression to what's happening internally, therefore they can represent fruition, the air element (communication and hearing), and the use of sacred sounds to improve personal awareness.

Spellworking for Smooth Operating Systems

Throughout your Web Witching, the last thing you'll want to experience are computer system glitches. These effectively "hang up" any energy that you were hoping to create until the problem is resolved. The purpose behind the following spells is to lend metaphysical support to maintenance procedures or routine safety precautions.

Antivirus Spell

Use this spell whenever you're scanning your system for viruses, or whenever you're loading in new virus software. Begin by making a small cup of soup into which you've placed a clean quartz crystal. Take this to your computer station and sit down. Stir the soup counterclockwise three times saying, *"Bugs and viruses, away away."* Then stir it clockwise three times, saying, *"Positive energy, stay stay."* Carefully spoon out the quartz, which has now absorbed the desired energy, dry it off, and leave it near your system. Drink the remaining soup while you work so that you internalize the positive vibrations and can therefore manifest more positive results.

Crash Guard

Use this spell when installing new electrical systems (like a new surge protector) or any crash guard software. Begin by finding a stone or other small token to represent your system, a small box, and some packing peanuts or dense foam. Keep the token near your system for at least a week so it attunes itself to your computer's vibrations. Then, just before the installation, take the box and put a few packing peanuts or the foam inside, making a little nest for the token.

As you put the token into the nest say, *"Safety surround, protection abound!"* Continue repeating the invocation while you finish packing

the token into the box so that it's immobilized. (This functions in the
same manner as the seat belt or airbag in your car, only on a metaphysical level.) Keep the box as close as possible to your hard drive
for ongoing protection. If your system ever crashes, you will need to
take this token out, break it, and create a new one. Breaking the token
releases back to the earth the negative energy it has accumulated.

Defragmentation

This spell is done in conjunction with a hard-drive cleanup. Begin
with a piece of square paper on which you've written the words "my
computer" (or, if you've named your system, put its name on the
paper). Next, during a waning moon, cut this paper into several
pieces, focusing on your intention to "cut away" any useless data or
unnecessary files. Wrap these pieces in a black cloth (for banishing)
until the next waxing to full moon.

Remove the pieces from their wrappings and bring them to the computer. Start the defragmentation process. Most systems will tell you the approximate time this will take. Divide the number of minutes by the number of paper pieces you have. Then, at even intervals, put the pieces back together, taping them securely or gluing them to a cardboard surface. If you wish, add an incantation or some supportive oils to the process (you can put the oil in the glue). This symbolically supports the restructuring of your system.

Techno-Thaw

This spell can be performed any time you're cleaning out old files from your drive, disks, e-mail, or whatever. The purpose of this spell is to help protect your system from freeze-ups, which are often caused by cluttered drives. It's incredibly simple, requiring only an ice cube, a bowl, a toothpick, and your computer!

Take the components to your computer altar. Write your wish for free-flowing energy on the ice cube using the toothpick. Visualize this being burned onto the ice with light-energy. Let the ice melt completely while you're working (if there's an area of your computer that generates heat, put the ice in the bowl there for best results). Then simply take the water outside and release it to the earth to keep your system's functions flowing unhindered.

Traveling Magic for Disks and Laptops

Since our society has become very mobile, there are likely to be times when you're traveling with a laptop or software and you want to make sure both continue to function effectively along the way. For this particular spell it's best to begin with your laptop's carrying case or a static-free bag for the software. Since both disks and computers can be categorized as "solar" objects, place the case or bag in sunlight for seven hours (the number of completion). The sun also has strong associations with safety, energy, and blessing.

Every hour, stop in front of the case/bag and say something like, "*As the sunlight pours down, operative power wraps around. Within this housing the magic's bound!*" When the seven hours are completed you can increase the power in the spell by placing a whole bay leaf inside a white cloth and adhering this to the case or bag somehow to absorb any problems or negative energy. If the bay leaf ever cracks, sprinkle the parts to the wind and replace it.

Antitheft Talisman for Laptops

To create this talisman you'll need one clove of garlic or a capsule of garlic, a tiny amethyst, a piece of coral, and a small pouch to place them in. Work during a waxing moon to augment growing protection or a dark moon to accent banishing unwanted interest. Take the bag to your computer altar with the stones and raise them up to the heavens saying, "*Magic here shine, this computer is mine. All thieves beware of this magical snare. Your intent, you will see, returns three by three.*"

Repeat this once each time for each item placed in the talisman, then immediately put the talisman inside your laptop's case. If at any time the garlic dries up or the coral chips, you'll need to replace them and reenergize the pouch.

All-purpose Protective Computer Charm

This is Trish's favorite spell. Fold a bay leaf in a static-free bag. In folk traditions, bay keeps "bugs" away from food, so why not your computer? For greater meaning, dab some sympathetic oils on the leaf or write your desire with the pointer finger of your strong hand on the leaf's surface. Keep your purpose strongly in mind, then place this under the monitor (adding an incantation if desired). Once a month remove the leaf, break it apart (which breaks up the negative energy it has collected), replace the leaf with a fresh one, and repeat the process.

Repair Spell

This spell is designed to help you send healing energy to your computer system and to know what to do about a nagging computer problem (even if that means calling in a repair person). Take a piece of paper and draw a simple depiction of your computer system on it. Turn the paper over and on it write these words three times: "Earth, Wind, Fire, and Sea, computer elementals speak to me. Find the problem, heal it quick, fix it now, with a click." Fold the paper in half and dab three drops of cedar or sage oil on it. Then fold it in half and then in half again, for a total of three times. Place the folded paper under the base of your computer monitor for three days. Every time you click on your system, see and sense the healing energy moving through it, healing it quick with a click.

Recovery Spell

This spell is designed to work in conjunction with the Undelete or Recover function of your system whereby a deleted file or file portion can be rescued. For this spell we'll be using an adaptation of an old folk spell designed to return lost items. For it you'll need a length of string and a piece of paper on which the name of the file is written.

Fold the paper three times then bind it with one end of the string. Place this bundle across the computer desk from you. Next, focus on the file's name, whispering it softly. Begin pulling on the string so the paper slowly comes toward you. When it's nearly in your hand, begin the recovery operation. Continue pulling the string while the computer works, and hold the paper tightly as the file or file portions come on the screen. Burn the paper and string afterward.

Online Spells

Your CPU has energy running through it the entire time the computer is on. Now you're going to be piggybacking magical energy through those energy lines to help in online Web Witching.

Message Spell

This spell is designed to add a specific energy signature to a message you're sending on the Net so the recipient doesn't misunderstand or misconstrue your meaning. Before getting online, make a tincture of rosemary (mental power) and basil (harmony). Keep this in a sealed container near the computer screen. Get online and type your message. Then put a little of the tincture on your fingertip (remember to close the container) and trace an invoking pentagram on the screen. If you wish, add an invocation at this point. When you're done drawing the image, click on "send" to literally send the energy you just illustrated!

Finding Spell

This is a quick spell designed to help make your surfing time more productive. Burn patchouli or vanilla incense to invite positive Web Witching energies. As the search engine comes up on the screen and you type in the appropriate keywords, say aloud three times, *"Cyber Goddess and Cyber God your guidance lend, show me who, what, where, how, why, and when. North, East, South, and West, show me which site is best."* Close your eyes for three seconds, and then open them and click on the very first site that you are drawn to on the screen.

File Transfer Spell

This spell is to protect the data as you download it or send it to someone else. Sirona likes to first download Web information onto a floppy disk instead of her hard disk as a precautionary measure and scanning out the data for viruses before dumping it onto her hard drive. When transferring files say aloud, *"Web Witching Wards and Watchtowers that be, stand guard while I surf the cyber sea. Transfer all Web files with speed and ease, with the blessings of the Cyber Gods, so mote it be."*

Web Resources for Spells

There are more and more Wiccan Web sites each day, and many of them offer a multitude of different spells and rituals for everything from love to banishment. To find these sites, first go to a search engine such as 37.com, altavista.com, or avatarsearch.com, and then type in keywords such as "pagan spells," "wicca spells," or "love spells." Click on the sites that offer what you are looking for. You may want to create your own Cyber Book of Shadows consisting of spells and rituals you have downloaded from pagan sites on the Internet. You can also add computer spells you collect along the way, such as the ones in this chapter. Be sure to consecrate the file or disk holding your Cyber Book of Shadows just as you would any other ritual object.

Spells Using the Computer as a Component

- *Banishing spell*   Use a disk with symbolic or literal information on it and then use a magnet to wipe that information out while visualizing moving the energy away from you.
- *Memory spell*   Use an old memory chip as portable magic to help you remember important things.
- *Luck turning*   Use an old mouse ball, turning it clockwise to "turn things around" and move them in a positive direction.
- *Web divination*   Hold a pendulum in one hand and get a baseline of "yes" and "no." Continue to hold the pendulum and use your other hand to control the mouse. Ask *"Which Web site is the best choice right now?"* (or whatever is appropriate to your needs), and then begin moving the cursor down the list of Web sites that come up on any search engine of sites. Stop on the site on which the pendulum swings "yes," and click.
- *Grounding*   Take an old disk and paint it the colors of the four elements in the correct quarters. Paint the center point black or

brown to represent earth. Carry this with you to keep you more strongly connected to terra firma. Whenever you're sitting down, put this under your feet for greater effectiveness.

- *Establishing or breaking connections*   Use two poppets made out of personal clothing and an old computer cable. Stuff each poppet with herbs suited to the reason for making or breaking the connection. For example, love connections might use rose petals, while a divorce situation might call for lily petals, which are used to dissipate love magic. The cable is used to loosely bind the poppets (so love doesn't constrain) or may be cut in two during the spell to sever connections. If you can't make poppets, paper dolls work, too.

- *Shapeshifting*   Use the disable and enable mouse option to help visualize yourself shapeshifting into a mouse and to shapeshift back into a human. As author Douglas Adams points out in *The Hitchhiker's Guide to the Galaxy*, the mice are the ones who are actually running this planet, so there's a lot we can learn from mouse-ness.

- *Spellcheck divination*   When you perform a spellcheck on a document, pay attention to the different word options that come up, and especially any personal associations you may have with these words. It's sort of like a Wiccan word association. Make a note of any magical or uncanny congruencies.

CYBER RITUALS

We perform rituals in our everyday life; they are things we do habitually, like using the same coffee cup or following the same morning routine. These little conventions give our lives a feeling of consistency and perpetuity, and are very comforting. Ever notice how out of sorts you feel when one of your daily rituals gets interrupted?

Wiccans perform magical rituals not only to honor or aid life's natural cycles; we also use rituals to keep our day-to-day reality as balanced as possible. With this in mind, you can see that Web Witching achieves this goal by using rituals that utilize the computer as an important participant in the rite. We may make use of the computer to send the cone of power raised in ritual where it needs to go. (How convenient that e-mail has a "send" button!) Rituals are performed to help the computer and its user in some way.

The Sacred Cyber Space

No matter what ritual you use, each begins similarly with the creation of sacred space. Simply defined, sacred space is a protective sphere of energy. Once inside this sphere our spirits have the capac-

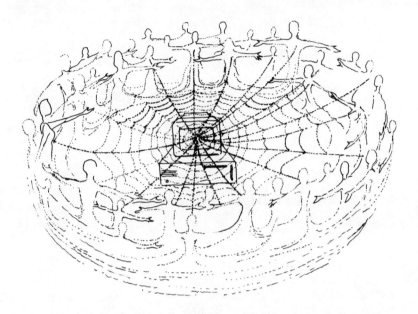

ity to work outside of space and time, touching the heart of what
magic truly is. This sphere holds our energy neatly in place, unhindered by unwanted outside interference, until we're ready to send it
on its way.

For the purpose of computer rituals, your computer altar
becomes the central point—a nucleus, if you will, around which the
ritual's words and actions will revolve. This is why it is important to
take care to set up your computer altar with tools, symbols, and
elemental components suited to the seasons, the space available, and
your path. They are about to become conduits for universal power
through which your magic will find meaning and manifestation.

Since we cannot possibly be aware of all the situations in your life
that may inspire a cyber ritual, we've decided to provide a few practical suggestions for creating your own sacred cyber space, as well as
a few theme-specific rituals for your use. As with all magical procedures, please make personally meaningful adjustments to these
examples so that the resulting rituals truly express your vision, and
are therefore more fulfilling.

Standard Elements of Ritual

PREPARATION   Gather together whatever items you'll need to perform the ritual effectively and place them on or around your computer altar. Make sure everything looks tidy, that there are no potentially damaging substances near your system, and that there is nothing to distract your attention from the task at hand.

TIMING   Timing will vary depending on the ritual's goal; however there are some good ways to use timing in your preparation process. For example, power up your computer at the first signs of dawn to signal the beginning of a magical day, then program it to be on stand-by until you're ready to start the ritual. (Note: this also starts the computer's fan running, which corresponds to the eastern-air element). For rituals dealing with banishing or endings, turn the machine on at dusk. For those meant to use the computer for divination or spirit contact, try the witching hour!

CALLING THE QUARTERS   Some traditions begin rituals by invoking the directions in the east, the place where the sun rises and a new day begins, and some in the north, the place of earth and spiritual origins. However, if it makes more sense to you, you may wish to begin in the south to honor the computer's fiery energy. Try this invocation.

EAST   *Winds of cooling and communication, I call and charge you. Move round this sacred space with the breeze of blessing.*

SOUTH   *Fires of transformation and power, I call and charge you. Ignite my system with the spark of magic.*

WEST   *Waters of intuition and cleansing, I call and charge you. Balance the fire in my heart with drops of wisdom and discernment.*

NORTH   *Soil of growth and maturity, I call and charge you. Keep the energy in this sacred space well grounded in reality and let it germinate in my heart.*

CENTER   *Binding tie of all things, I call and invite you to join this circle. In this moment beyond space and time, let spirit and technology find a meeting ground in which magic will be born and manifested. So be it.*

OPENING THE CIRCLE   Invocation is part of opening, but there is more to it than that. The opening of any ritual prepares the participants (even if its a gathering of one) for magic. It sets the ambiance and tone, and helps you turn your thoughts away from the temporal toward the spiritual. Patterned breathing, chants, music, and other similar activities can aid in achieving this goal.

RITUAL BODY   This should include any spells, meditations, songs, and other activities designed to accent the theme of the observance and build power to support your goals.

CLOSING THE CIRCLE   This includes a dismissal of the circle and other activities aimed at bringing people back into touch with the real world, like a closing prayer and postritual feasting.

RITE OF WEB WITCHING

This ritual should be done before you go online to network with other like-minded people. With this ritual, you will create an atmosphere in and around your computer and yourself that will support and guide your efforts.

NECESSARY COMPONENTS   A dream-catcher or a picture of a spider-web, a carnelian stone (for effective communication), a piece of yellow string, sandalwood incense, and a gold candle. (Note: If incense or smudge smoke bothers you, use a diffuser or a few drops of oil in a cup of hot water to get the scents-ual effect.)

INVOCATION AND OPENING   Call the quarters and open the circle using the directions given previously in this chapter. Light the candle and incense. Anoint yourself with the oil.

RITUAL BOON   Take the string and begin weaving it though the dream-catcher or wrapping it around the picture while saying

Come Cyber Goddesses of Earth and Air
Come Cyber Goddesses of Water and Fire
Come now and hear our prayers.

Come Cyber Gods of Earth and Air
Come Cyber Gods of Water and Fire
Come now and hear our prayers.

Weave a Wiccan Web of peace, love, and light
Make it strong and wise and make it bright.

Weave a Wiccan Web of peace, love, and light
Connect us together in One infinite megabyte.

Weave a Wiccan Web of peace, love, and light
Protect it all day and each and every night.

Forever and ever, so be it! Blessed Be!

CLOSING THE CIRCLE   Place the dream-catcher or picture on your computer altar when you are done weaving. Keep the carnelian stone on your computer altar to remind you that you are now a part of the whole Wiccan Web. Turn on your computer and surf for a while. When you are done, thank the gods and goddesses for their presence and help, and release the circle.

POSTRITUAL ACTIVITIES   Keep surfing!

PROTECTING YOUR PERSONAL WEB PAGE OR DOMAIN

As you know there are always little glitches (and some big glitches) when working with computers and the Internet. Viruses, crashes, and spam are all real risks you expose yourself and your computer to when you surf the Web. The following ritual is designed to keep these cyber plagues at bay.

NECESSARY COMPONENTS   A piece of malachite or, better yet, a malachite pyramid, three bay leaves, dragon's blood oil, smudge made from sage, cedar, and sweetgrass, and a white candle.

INVOCATION AND OPENING   Call the quarters and open the circle. Light the candle and use the candle flame to light the smudge. Smudge yourself in the smoke and then anoint yourself with the oil.

RITUAL BODY

> *Goddess and God protect my system and me*
> *From all cyber harm, invisible and seen.*
> *Energize the cyber magic and set it free*
> *Bringing its powerful wisdom to me.*
>
> *Oh Kerridwen, Great Mother of darkness and light*
> *Keep the cyber circle open and keep it bright.*
> *Oh Kernunnos, Great Father of life and power*
> *Protect my system from viruses and guard my tower.*
>
> *Bless this computer in your sacred name*
> *And never let its power wane.*
> *Ayea, Ayea, Ayea!*

CLOSING THE CIRCLE   Thank the goddesses and gods for their presence, help, and protection. When you are done, allow the candle and incense to burn down completely. Release the circle.

POSTRITUAL ACTIVITIES   Put the bay leaves under your tower to protect it. Keep the piece of malachite permanently on your computer altar as a cyber amulet. Make sure your files are updated, you disks put away, and remember, always back up your files!

Cyber Rituals for the Sabbats

The Sabbats allow us to attune ourselves to the reoccurring cycles of birth, life, death, and rebirth, and to become aware of the circular flow inherent in everything. The Sabbats also celebrate the God and Goddess as they progress through the wheel of the seasons.

   Knowing the exact astrological time of the Sabbats gives you the advantage in any magical work because this is when the powers are most opportune for gathering, moving, and manifesting magical energy on the Internet and elsewhere. Use an ephemeris to pinpoint the exact time of the Sabbats, which are based on eight equal divisions of the solar year. There are also many pagan sites that list the day and time for you. Wiccans often perform Sabbat rituals on the eve of the Sabbat; others conduct their rituals at different times during the day.

When working as a solitary Web Witch, you don the roles of both the Goddess and God in ritual. Keep in mind that you can work with a partner or even a group of people when Web Witching. The following procedures are adapted from Celtic Druid tradition, and so the Celtic pantheon of gods and goddesses are featured. You can easily change pantheons, modifying the rituals accordingly. Remember these rituals are provided to give you framework from which you can work.

Begin by setting up your computer altar.

DRAWING THE SACRED CYBER CIRCLE   The circle is drawn as a means of protection from negative influences during rituals. Keep in mind that you can create a virtual altar on your computer screen and move your cursor in a clockwise circle over the appropriate quadrant while chanting. Virtual altars and sacred cyber spaces are especially useful for those practitioners who require secrecy. Creating a virtual altar and using virtual tools allows you to practice without anyone knowing you are doing so—keeping your spirituality alive and strong while developing your magical skills.

Sit (desk chair that swivels is handy here) or stand in front of your computer altar. Breathe deeply and then begin to see or sense a clear, cobalt-blue light washing out the area around you as you say, "May all evil and foulness be gone from my computer and this sacred cyber space. I ask this in the Lady's name. Be gone, now and forever more." Do this three times while turning clockwise. If you are sitting in a swivel chair, just spin around clockwise. If you are using a virtual altar, move your mouse in a clockwise circle, energetically connecting the four points (north, east, south, and west), while visualizing a sphere of cobalt-blue light surrounding you and protecting you. You can also think the incantation to yourself.

With your athame, hand, or mouse, draw an energetic circle around your sacred cyber space by visualizing a blue-white flame beaming from the tip of your athame blade, your fingertips, or the mouse pointer as it moves around the four corners of your virtual ritual space.

Purify the four corners of your sacred cyber space by starting at the north point and chanting, *"Ayea, Ayea Kerridwen! Ayea, Ayea Kernunnos! Ayea, Ayea, Ayea!"* After purifying the North point, continue on to the East, South and West points. You can roll to the appropriate corners if you are sitting on a swivel chair and space allows for it. If doing a virtual ritual, move the mouse pointer over the appropriate corners while chanting.

Face your computer altar (the monitor) and say in a firm voice, *"Blessed be! Blessed be the gods! Blessed be all who are gathered here."*

Merge with the Goddess and God by allowing yourself to become one with all things. Say aloud, *"I am the Goddess, the Goddess is me, we are one. I am the God, the God is me, we are one. I am my computer, my computer is me, we are one. I am the Web, the Web is me, we are one."*

Gently knock a total of nine times in three series of three on your computer altar either with the handle of your athame, the bottom of your wand (pen or pencil), your knuckles, or the bottom edge of your mouse. Your Sacred Cyber Circle is now set in place until you release it.

CALLING THE CYBER WARDS   After you set the Sacred Cyber Circle in place, the time has come to call in the Cyber Wards to stand guard at each of the four corners during ritual. This procedure is tailored for your computer space and the objects on hand. You will need a paper clip holder and three paper clips, a letter opener or scissors, a small lit white candle in a holder or a small penlight flashlight, and a glass or cup of water. Sirona suggests sitting in a swivel chair or standing while calling in the Cyber Wards.

Once your Sacred Cyber Circle is drawn, the altar tools are brought into the center of the circle. These can be physical or virtual tools.

Take your bowl or holder filled with paper clips and, facing your computer altar (the north point), lay three paper clips carefully on the altar.

Set the bowl or paper clip holder down on your altar and, holding your letter opener or scissors in your right hand and lifting both of your arms above your head, say aloud, *"Oh, great and mighty one, Ruler of the North Cyber March, Come, I pray you. Protect the servers of the North Cyber Ward. Come, I summon you!"*

Set your letter opener or scissors on the altar.

Take up your pen or pencil and face the East point, or move your cursor to the East quadrant of your virtual altar. Wave your pen or pencil three times to the left and then three times to the right and then set it down on your altar. Pick up your letter opener or scissors in your right hand, hold up your arms and say, *"Oh, great and mighty one, Ruler of the East Cyber March, Come, I pray you. Protect the servers of the East Cyber Ward. Come, I summon you!"*

Set down your letter opener or scissors.

Take the lit candle or penlight and face the South point, or move your cursor to the South point. Wave the candle or flashlight three times across the South point. Set the candle or flashlight down carefully on your altar, a safe distance from your hardware, and with your letter opener or scissors in your right hand, hold your arms upward and say, *"Oh great and mighty one, Ruler of the South Cyber March, Come, I pray you. Protect the servers of the South Cyber Ward. Come, I summon you!"*

Set down your letter opener or scissors on the altar.

Take the glass of water and face the West point. Dab three drops of water on your computer altar, and set the glass back down on your altar. Hold your letter opener or scissors in your right hand, and with your arms upward, say, *"Oh great and mighty one, Ruler of the West Cyber March, Come, I pray you. Protect the servers of the West Cyber Ward. Come, I summon you!"*

Set down your letter opener or scissors on your computer altar. The four Cyber Wards are now standing guard.

Face your computer altar and begin to chant the names of your favorite goddesses and gods. For example, *"Kerridwen, Kerridwen, Kerridwen, Kernunnos, Kernunnos, Kernunnos, Ayea, Ayea, Ayea!"* Build the power up and then direct the energy toward the magical work at hand. Swiveling around clockwise or standing and swaying back and forth enhances the final power buildup.

CUTTING THE LITTLE CYBER GATE   After the Four Cyber Wards are called into your Sacred Cyber Space, it's time to cut the Little Cyber Gate, which is an energetic gate or doorway in the East quadrant. When you need to move out of your Sacred Cyber Space for any reason, for example to change the music or get snacks, you go through the Little Cyber Gate, using the tip of your athame or letter opener or scissors to cut it in a clockwise manner, starting at the bottom left point of the door. Once you are back within your Sacred Cyber Circle, be sure to close the Cyber Gate by using your athame and starting at the right bottom point of the door or gate, moving up, across to top, and then down to the left bottom point.

VIRTUAL TOASTING   After Sabbat and Esbat rituals, Wiccans fill their glasses with drink and select their favorite goddesses and gods and propose a toast to them. For instance, raise your glass and say, "To Lugh, Ayea master craftsman and lover!" or "To Anu, Great Mother of abundance, healing, and wisdom," or "Ayea Dagda, the Good God!"

Sirona uses toasting as a means of connecting her own energy with that of the goddesses and gods. By connecting to these divine energies, I bring them into my life and honor them as my family and friends. I also like to honor divine beings such as Buddha, Bast, and Odin from other spiritual paths. I find this completely in tune with the spirit of the tradition because Wicca is inclusive rather than exclusive and encourages innovation and creativity.

When surfing on the Wiccan Web and doing Sabbat and Esbat cyber rituals, you can also use graphics to create a virtual toasting environment on your desktop. Search for graphics of elegant or funky chalices that you like and import them into an appropriate program.

VIRTUAL FEASTING   Along with toasting, feasts are a common custom after Sabbat rituals. The feast is a sacred meal in honor of the Goddess and God. In the Celtic tradition, feasting is considered to be one of the gifts the Dagda, the Good God, gave to humankind.

The feast begins immediately after the main body of Sabbat and Esbat rituals, before the circle is released. Prepare a special meal for yourself—something you can set on your computer altar and nibble on. Feasting and toasting are ways of expressing yourself and connecting the physical with the ethereal.

Virtual feasting, like virtual toasting, can be done with virtual foods, which is a great way to keep those extra pounds off! Sirona prefers real foods over virtual foods because of the sensual pleasure of eating, but in a pinch, virtual feasting may fit your needs.

During the feast Sirona encourages you to add music (many audio clips are available on the Web), poems, and divination experiences (see chapter 7 for online divination sites). All of these things can be accessed on the Wiccan Web.

Feasting is the perfect time to promote your spiritual growth and develop your magical skills by exploring Wicca, metaphysics, and the concept of Oneness. So when we suggest you toast and feast after the main body of each Sabbat ritual, we mean you should go ahead and get on the Web and surf around, checking out sites of interest that may increase your magical skills and deepen your understanding of Oneness.

This is also a good time to make a note of any Goddess and God dreams and visitations, insights, synchronicities, and messages, keying the details into a computer file for your easy reference.

RELEASING THE CIRCLE   When you have finished your work, release the circle turning counterclockwise and visualizing the blue-white flame you imagined while casting the circle being sucked back into the tip of your athame blade, your fingertips, or the cursor as it moves around the four corners of your virtual cyber ritual space. Finally, knock three times on your computer altar either with the handle of your athame (or letter opener), the bottom of your wand or pen or pencil, your knuckles, or the bottom edge of your mouse.

The Wheel of the Year

The following rituals are for each Sabbat of the Wiccan year and use easy-to-find components. While doing the rituals, hold the suggested stone in your dominant hand whenever possible or place it on the altar to charge it with magical energy. We advise keeping your charged stones away from your hard drive or computer monitor because they can influence and generate magnetic fields. Keep the stones from each ritual on your computer altar as a reminder of your connection to the Wiccan Web and the Cyber God and Goddess.

At the very beginning of each ritual, before you draw your Sacred Cyber Circle and call in the Cyber Wards, gather together all the supplies you will need, and place a copy of the ritual conveniently in front of you. Remember, feel free to adapt the rituals to fit your needs.

Prepare yourself for the Cyber Sabbat Rituals by anointing yourself with the suggested oil. Do so by dabbing a drop of oil on your third eye, on the back of your head, behind each ear, and on the inside of your wrists and ankles. Use a small bowl or small cauldron to hold any loose herbs, and place this bowl on your computer altar. Next, light the suggested incense and candle. Be sure to dedicate the lighting of each to the goddess or god of your choice. Make an effort to match the appropriate goddess and god to the seasonal celebration.

Finally, turn on your computer, which is an important component of the ritual. Sirona likes to scan pictures that match the Sabbat into her desktop view, creating a great visual for her to focus on during rituals. Then she sets her Scrolling Marquee screen saver to come on after three minutes, so it appears at the beginning of the ritual. She uses part of the ritual and the names of her favorite goddesses and gods as Scrolling Marquee type, which reinforces the focus of the ritual at hand.

SAMHAIN (HALLOWEEN)

NECESSARY COMPONENTS   Bloodstone, nine cloves, and a cinnamon stick (or pinch of ground cinnamon), sandalwood incense, carnation oil, and a red candle.

INVOCATION AND OPENING   Draw the Sacred Cyber Circle and call in the Cyber Wards.

RITUAL BODY   Say the following words:

By moonshine the animals sing
By starlight, the owl does wing
Across the window of the Web
Gliding into the timeless ebb.

The Lord and Lady interact and rest awhile
Connecting the seasons, transferring files.
Reflecting Life, Death, and Rebirth
May they guide me whenever I surf.

Oh computer, Cauldron of Creation
Weave a bright web for my navigation
Help me search and find nature's key
In everything I sense and see.

Ayea Morrigan!
Ayea Dagda!
Ayea, Ayea, Ayea!

CLOSING CIRCLE   Perform any magical works you may have planned at this point. Toast the gods and feast if you like, with real or virtual food and drink. After you are done, thank the Goddess and God for their presence and then release the circle. Allow the candle and incense to burn down completely. Lastly, turn off your computer and put any ritual tools away.

POSTRITUAL ACTIVITIES   Take the nine cloves and the cinnamon stick and put them in a red pouch or in a square piece of red fabric, and then tie it up with a red ribbon or string. Keep this Samhain bag on or near your computer altar as a symbol of renewal.

WINTER SOLSTICE (YULE)

This Yule ritual should begin just before midnight and the words "Blessed be, Blessed be, Blessed be the Gods!" should ideally be spoken no more than three minutes after midnight. After this, spin clockwise several times either in a swivel chair or standing, all the while sensing a building up of divine energies. As you come to a rest, direct this built-up energy toward a specific magical work or desire, for example, world peace.

NECESSARY COMPONENTS   A clear quartz crystal, three bay leaves, lavender oil, a pinecone (real or virtual), frankincense and myrrh incense, and a white candle.

INVOCATION AND OPENING   Draw the Sacred Cyber Circle and call the Cyber Wards.

RITUAL BODY   Say the following words:

In the frozen silence, Nature holds her breath
Singing silent songs of Rebirth, Life, and Death.
The snow covers the Mother in a glistening cloak of white
Stars like snowflakes glitter in the stillness of the night.

Merging with wonder and oneness, I click on home
As the Cyber Goddess and God celebrate and set the tone.
Reprogramming the settings, they ready themselves for spring
Turning the Universal Wheel and reconnecting the Magical Ring.

Rejoicing and rebooting the forms and forces Divine
The Goddess and God plug in and animate nine times nine.
Humming bold cyber tunes of holiday love, peace, and joy
Bringing magical Web gifts to every girl and every boy.

Blessed be, Blessed be, Blessed be the gods!

CLOSING THE CIRCLE   Do any magical work you may have designated for this Sabbat. This is a good time to initiate any projects or to start building your Web page if you haven't already done so. Give yourself any Yule gifts you may have planned, such as new software or perhaps a Celtic-theme mousepad. Send a few virtual Yule cards to special friends. Toast the goddesses and gods and feast, with real or virtual food and drink. After you are done, thank the Goddess and God for their presence and then release the circle. Allow the candle and incense to burn down completely.

POSTRITUAL ACTIVITIES   Place the three bay leaves (for protection and clarity) under your tower and keep the pinecone (if real) on your computer altar. If you used a virtual pinecone, you can include it in your Yule desktop or on your virtual altar. The pinecone represents the fertile Goddess.

IMBOLC (BRIDGET'S DAY, CANDLEMAS)

NECESSARY COMPONENTS   An amethyst, lavender oil, a pinch of rosemary, vanilla incense, and a yellow or gold candle. (Wait to light the candle until indicated in the ritual.)

INVOCATION AND OPENING   Draw the Sacred Cyber Circle and Call the Cyber Wards.

RITUAL BODY   Say the following words:

Bridget, Bridget, Bridget!
Brightest flame!
Bridget, Bridget, Bridget!
Sacred name!

Oh great Bridget, I come to ask this gift of you
I ask the gift of thy presence in my computer and heart
Lady of Wisdom, keep my hardware and software true
Beloved Mother protect me when I shut down and restart.

Bridget, Bridget, Bridget!
Brightest flame!
Bridget, Bridget, Bridget!
Sacred name!

[Light the candle now]

She comes!
Blessed be the bride of earth, air, fire, and sea!
Beloved Mother Bridget, we praise and thank thee!
As the Lady of the Sacred Fire wills, so mote it be!

CLOSING THE CIRCLE   Do any magical work you may have planned. Toast the goddesses and gods and feast. After you are done, thank the goddess Bridget for her divine presence and invite her to remain in your heart, computer tower, and home forever and a day. Thank any other divine beings and cyber friends that may have been present in your Cyber Circle and then release the circle. Allow the candle and incense to burn down completely.

POSTRITUAL ACTIVITIES   Take the rosemary and scatter it just outside your front door to invite the presence of the goddess Bridget into your home for the coming year.

SPRING EQUINOX (HERTHA'S DAY, THE LADY'S DAY)

NECESSARY COMPONENTS   Malachite, a packet of seeds, lavender oil, jasmine incense, and a green candle.

INVOCATION AND OPENING   Draw the Sacred Cyber Circle and call the Cyber Wards.

Ritual Body   Say the following words:

Hear now, all of the wonders of Nature's song
Birds call, bees buzz, and crickets sing along.
Bright is the day and the morning is sweet
It's time for Blessed be and merry meet.

The Lord of the Forests does frolic and run
Linking his forward steps with the sun.
The Lady of the Lake does awaken and arise
Weaving the Web with love in her eyes.

Gathering together are animals large and small
Flowers open, dragonflies dance, see them all.
Trees dance in threes, in pairs, in unison
And evening stars bloom with the setting sun.

The Web Circle of Life continues to thrive
Once again the whole of existence comes alive.
I link to the Mother, I link to the Sun
I am the Solar Webmaster, I am the Golden One!

Hold the packet of seeds between both of your hands and visualize the positive growing energy of the spring sun filling the seeds as you say three times, "*I am the Solar Webmaster, I am the Golden One!*" Continue to hold the seeds between your hands for a minute or two, until your hands begin feeling hot. Then place the seeds on your computer altar for the duration of the ritual.

Closing the Circle   Do any magical work you may have planned. Toast the gods and feast if you like, with real or virtual food and drink. After you are done, thank the Goddess and God for their help and release the circle. Allow the candle and incense to burn down completely.

Postritual Activities   Take the packet of seeds and plant them somewhere they will grow strong and healthy.

BELTANE (MAY DAY)

NECESSARY COMPONENTS   An aventurine stone, mint leaves, jasmine incense, ylang-ylang oil, two nuts (such as almonds or cashews), a green candle placed on the left side of your computer altar and a red candle placed on the right side. Crush the mint leaves between your fingers just before the ritual so the scent is on your hands. Keep the crushed leaves in a small bowl.

INVOCATION AND OPENING   Draw the Sacred Cyber Circle and call the Cyber Wards.

RITUAL BODY   Say the following words:

Behold! See the Golden One dancing
Out of the East he comes a-prancing
Bringing a full-screen greening treat
To every cyber woman and man he meets.

The adventure of the sun is on hand
Hearts sing out across cyber land
All acts of pleasure, laughter, and love
Sweetly remind us that as below, so above.

The magic has been passed down for us to learn
Love and magic fill the Web as the seasons turn.
So let's surf the Web for a golden year and a day
Now is the time to joyfully play! Ayea, Ayea, Ayea!

CLOSING THE CIRCLE   Do any magical work—keep in mind that Beltane is a fertility Sabbat, and is a powerful time to begin any new project or creation. Toast the gods and feast. Surf around a bit and check out some of the more Beltane-themed sites. You might even find a virtual maypole or two you can dance around! After you are done, thank the Goddess and God for their presence and release the circle. Allow the candles and incense to burn down completely.

POSTRITUAL ACTIVITIES   Take the nuts and mint leaves and put them in a small green pouch or tie them up in a small green cloth with a green ribbon or string. Hang the bag from your desk lamp with a gold or yellow ribbon

SUMMER SOLSTICE (MIDSUMMER, LETHA'S DAY)

NECESSARY COMPONENTS   A moonstone, a fresh rose, a pinch of thyme, honeysuckle oil, rose incense, an apple (preferably a golden one), and a yellow or gold candle. Using a clean letter opener or your athame, slice the apple in half widthwise to reveal the pentacle of seeds inside of it. Place the two halves on a piece of clean white paper on your computer altar. Put the rose in the glass of water in a safe place on your altar, preferably in close proximity to your monitor, so you can see it when you are working on your computer.

INVOCATION AND OPENING   Draw the Sacred Cyber Circle and call the Cyber Wards.

RITUAL BODY

> On the long summer's day, you meet a lovely Lady
> Dressed in bright silver, dressed in gray.
>
> She, with sweetest smile, bids you to sleep awhile
> To rest awhile in Her land as she calls up your file.
>
> She is Rhiannon, Lady of Avalon, Lady of rest,
> Lady of the Golden Apples in the Land of the Blest.
>
> With a smile, she hands you a beautiful flower
> Its bloom and scent its soul and power.
>
> Then She gives you a sweet golden apple to eat
> And you start feeling a strange coldness in your feet.
>
> With a smile, She gives you another that is sweeter still
> It tastes so good, but the coldness shuts down your will.

She gives you a third, and it tastes sweeter than the second
But the coldness is so great, even more than you reckoned.

She tells you "For nine months of each year here you will be
But for three months, you shall stay in Avalon with me."

So when the sun is at its fullest, on this particular day
And you see a lovely Lady dressed in silver and in gray.

Welcome her with open arms as she responds in kind
Accessing the Goddess comm central of your mind.

Ayea Rhiannon, Ayea, Ayea, Ayea!

CLOSING THE CIRCLE   Take the rose out of the glass of water and drip three drops of water on the surface of each of the apple halves, tracing the pentacle on the apple halves with the stem of the rose. Place the rose back in the glass. Slice a tiny piece of apple from each half and set these tiny pieces aside in the bowl with the pinch of thyme. Eat the apple halves slowly and mindfully, savoring them as you do.

Do any magical work you have planned. Toast the gods and feast. After you are done, thank the goddess Rhiannon and any other goddesses and gods for their divine presence and help; then release the circle. Allow the candles and incense to burn down completely.

POSTRITUAL ACTIVITIES   Keep the rose next to your computer for a few days until it starts to wither. Put the rose in the bowl with the pinch of thyme and tiny apple pieces and allow them all to dry out completely. When dry, place all of the contents of the bowl into a golden pouch or into a small square of gold or yellow cloth tied up with a gold or yellow ribbon or string. Place this outside on a small stick in your flower garden, in a potted plant, or in a flower box, or you can tie it to a bird feeder.

LUGHNASSAD (LAMMAS)

NECESSARY COMPONENTS   A citrine, rose oil, vanilla incense, a red or orange candle, and a chocolate bar divided into eight pieces. This ritual is more fun to do with a partner, but can also be enjoyed alone. I also suggest you scan, cut and paste, or copy a picture of a cornucopia (horn of plenty) overflowing with vegetables, fruits, grains, software, chocolate, and other favorite things and use it on your desktop view, and set the screensaver to come on after thirty minutes (or turning it off completely), so the image will be on the screen for the entire ritual. Another suggestion is to set your Scrolling Marquee to toast the Goddess and God (Ayea Lugh, Ayea Rosemerta, Ayea, Ayea, Ayea!). You can also create a Lughnassad screen saver with animated cornucopia and other symbols of abundance and plenty.

INVOCATION AND OPENING   Draw the Sacred Cyber Circle and call the Cyber Wards.

RITUAL BODY   Say the following words:

> Hear me now, Great Creative One,
> Long-Hand Lugh of the Cyber Arts
> Grant me now with your loving presence
> Oh Master Craftsman of our hearts.

> Hear me now Great Abundant One
> Lovely Rose Mother, Lady of Light
> Grant me now divine access to the Web
> In the light of day or dark of night.

Take the pieces of chocolate (four each if you are working with a partner), hold them up toward the north, and say with passion in your voice,

> Ayea! Ayea! Rosemerta!
> Ayea! Ayea! Lugh!
> Ayea! Ayea! Ayea!

Turn (or swivel) to the east and do the same: likewise to the south and west directions. Then turn toward your computer altar again. Take one piece of chocolate and place it in your partner's mouth while saying,

Great, Mighty, and Sweetest Ones
Let Thy Blessing and Power
Enter into this chocolate!
So mote it be!

Have your partner do the same to you, repeating the previous words.

Continue doing this until you have eaten all of the chocolate. If you are working alone, repeat the saying just before you put the piece of chocolate in your mouth (a total of eight times).

Finally, face your computer altar and say loudly and firmly,

Blessed be the cyber God and Goddess,
Blessed be the providers, servers, and users!
Blessed be all who are gathered here!
Blessed be!

CLOSING THE CIRCLE Keep in mind that this is one of the best Sabbats for handfasting and craft marriage, so perform any loving nuptials at this time. If you have a divine or faery lover, this is the time to honor her or him. Do any magical work you may have planned. Toast the gods and goddesses and feast. After you are done, thank the god Lugh and the goddess Rosemerta for their presence and release the circle. Allow the candle and incense to burn down completely.

POSTRITUAL ACTIVITIES Lovemaking, reading a romance novel, or watching a steamy video (like *Sirens*) is encouraged after the Lughnassad ritual. Also you may want to check out some of the sex magic or some of the more tasteful sex-themed sites on the Web.

VERNAL EQUINOX (HELLITH'S DAY)

NECESSARY COMPONENTS A carnelian, patchouli oil, a pinch of vervain, balsam fir or sage incense, and an orange candle.

INVOCATION AND OPENING Draw the Sacred Cyber Circle and call the Cyber Wards.

RITUAL BODY   Say the following words:

Listen to the sound of the baying hounds
When the sun is both dark and most bright
In this season of change and seduction
When the moon embraces the sun's light.

When daytime and nighttime are equal
It is time to live, die, and be reborn
I link with Cyber Spirit and life immortal
To continue the circle just as I have sworn.

The password is spoken once again
It is perfect peace, trust, and love
I call out in this the twilight of the seasons
Hidden 'neath the mantle of cloak and glove.

In cyber circles of servers, modems, and users
Install, connect, and join the Web dance
In Faery circles of oak, hawthorn, and ash
It's time to sing and spin and take a chance.

Dressed in autumn fire and ablaze with joy
Come dance with me and I'll dance with you
Samewise and sunwise to center, in and out
Come dance with me and I'll dance with you!

Merry meet, merry part, and merry meet again!
Ayea, Ayea, Ayea!

CLOSING THE CIRCLE   This is an excellent time for initiations and works that require rebirth, renewal, or remodeling. Toast the gods, feast, and thank them for their gifts and for the harvests you have experienced through the year. Thank the Goddess and God for their presence in your cyber circle. After have completed your ritual, release the circle. Allow the candle and incense to burn down completely.

POSTRITUAL ACTIVITIES   Take the vervain, hold it in your hands, and make a wish, then scatter the herbs just outside your front door and let the wind carry them away.

Cyber Esbat (Full Moon) Celebrations

The moon rules the tides and guides the ebb and flow of magical energies. The waxing moon is best for starting new projects, accelerating personal growth, and building magical power. The three days after the new moon are optimum for beginning projects that will come to fruition during the full moon. The days just before the full moon are the best during which to complete projects because of the high amount of universal energy available at that time. The full or high moon is generally the best time for healing rituals. The waning moon and black (new) moon are best for banishing negativity, neutralizing enemies, and removing harmful influences or obstacles in your life. The first quarter is the point halfway between the new moon and the full moon, while the last quarter is the midpoint between the full and new moon.

The Wiccan Days of Power are the Sabbats plus the 13 full moons in a year. (Esbats). You can pinpoint the exact time of each full moon with an ephemeris. Many calendars now list the new moon, first quarter, full moon, and last quarter. Full moon rituals should usually be performed on the night closest to the actual full moon, preferably during the exact time the moon is full or while the moon is still waxing.

The cycle begins with the first full moon after Yule.

MOON NAME	COLOR	GEMSTONES
1. Wolf	Gray	Moonstone
2. Storm	Black	Onyx or Obsidian
3. Chaste	Green	Aventurine
4. Seed	Brown	Malachite
5. Hare	Pink	Rose Quartz
6. Dyad	Red	Ruby or Garnet
7. Mead	Green	Malachite
8. Wort	Yellow	Golden Topaz
9. Barley	Brown	Carnelian

10.	Wine	Purple	Amethyst
11.	Blood	Blue	Lapis
12.	Snow	White	Clear Quartz or Diamond
13.	Oak*	Gold	Amber (a hard resin) or Pyrite

*Note: The Oak moon is not celebrated during years that have only 12 moons.

FULL MOON HEALING RITUAL

This ritual can be used for yourself or for others. How often have you been far away from someone who had a pressing physical illness and wished desperately that there was something you could do to help? Well, there is, if that person or someone they know is hooked up to the Internet! By connecting with them through an instant-messenger type program or by sending them an e-mail near the end of the ritual, you can release your cone of healing power into the Web. They then receive it by answering the message or opening the file!

NECESSARY COMPONENTS   Use the color and stone associated with the moon during which you are doing the Healing Ritual (see the chart above). Burn sage and cedar smudge and light a white or silver candle. Anoint yourself with honeysuckle or amber oil.

INVOCATION AND OPENING   Draw the Sacred Cyber Circle and call the Cyber Wards. Draw a second circle of Sacred Fire on top of the Sacred Cyber Circle using your athame or letter opener.

RITUAL BODY
    See and sense the person to be healed. Scan in or download a photo of the person to be healed and call it up on your screen to focus on during the ritual. Next, see and sense a wave of cobalt-blue light washing out your entire being. This removes all negative energies. Next wash the image on your computer screen with cobalt-blue light, either energetically or by changing the image color to blue. Then repeat the procedure using green light (for healthy new

growth), changing it into gold light (to fuel the healing). Then face your computer screen and say:

> I call upon the three faces of the Goddess
> Maiden, Mother, and Crone
> I call upon the three faces of the God
> Son, Father, and Wise One
> Bless and heal (say the name of the person to be healed) on this eve
> Let all illness be cast from (person's name)
> These divine gifts from you I ask and pray
> Take all the pain and sickness away
> By the powers of Earth, Sky, and Sea
> Blessed be! So mote it be!

Visualize and breathe in healing white light from all around you into the person being healed and into the image on the screen. Breathe the white light in above, below, before, behind, and within you, to your left and to your right. Do this for at least five minutes.

CLOSING THE CIRCLE   Thank the Goddess and God for their presence and healing gifts. Put everything away and release the circle.

POSTRITUAL ACTIVITIES   Create a file containing an image of the person you did the healing work for, and add healing symbols and colors to the image. Save the file and keep it if you were the one to be healed, or e-mail it to the person you did the healing for.

Online Cyber Rituals

Holding rituals online is a little different than doing them yourself or with others in your own home, because you're going to be linking up with individuals in the magical community around the globe in order to produce magic aimed at mutual goals. This is very exciting! It adds so much more power to your effort, encourages fellowship, and promotes tolerance, understanding, and respect.

However, there are some important factors you'll need to consider in setting up online rituals.

- Make sure that everyone involved won't be cut off during the ritual (that they have sufficient server time available).
- Take into account the time differences from one area or country to another so that everyone can be working at the same time and be able to follow the ritual on their computer screens together (like a mini-chat).
- E-mail each participant an outline of the ritual beforehand so they all can gather what they need to participate in the rite. Be sure to leave sufficient time for feedback and changes. People should always alert one another of any personal variations in ritual components or tools, as this can shift the energies somewhat.
- Allow sufficient time in between each part of the ritual for people to share thoughts or feelings as inspired by Spirit. You also need to leave sufficient time so people can ready themselves and their cyber altar for the next part.
- Leave ample time at the end of the ritual for online fellowship and reflection. How was this effort successful? Who felt what (and when)? What might you keep or change in the future? This kind of discussion not only internalizes the energy of the cyber ritual but will provide you with the foundations for your next effort.

The cyber rituals that follow are only ideas; there are many more that you can create for yourself. Most of the rituals are tailored for chat rooms, except for the Forgiveness and Peace Ritual, which is to be done by two people, preferably with an instant-messenger type link.

RITUAL OF UNITY AND SUPPORT

The one thing the Wiccan community can always use a little more of is unified action, thought, and supportive magic. Since we follow a belief system that is not mainstream, there are times when we all feel overwhelmed, lonely, and just want to connect with someone who feels the same way we do. The Internet allows us to find comrades and reach out with a mystical cyber salve.

NECESSARY COMPONENTS   Lavender oil, two paper clips, vanilla incense, a white candle, and a pinch of rosemary.

INVOCATION AND OPENING   All participants should gather together in a chat room at an agreed upon day and time and decide which person will be the leader of the ritual. Light the incense and candle, and then anoint yourself with the lavender oil. Put the two paper clips and the rosemary in a small bowl on your computer altar next to the candle. Draw your Sacred Cyber Circle and call the Cyber Wards. The leader should then begin to type in the ritual words found below. (An option you can try is for each person to take a line of the ritual and type it in at the appropriate time. Then everyone gets to participate.)

RITUAL BODY   The leader types:

> *We call upon all of our Cyber friends*
> *And invite them to click on now!*
> *We call upon the Cyber Spirits of Earth*
> *And invite them to click on now!*
> *We call upon the Cyber Spirits of Air*
> *And invite them to click on now!*
> *We call upon the Cyber Spirits of Fire*
> *And invite them to click on now!*
> *We call upon the Cyber Spirits of Water*
> *And invite them to click on now!*
>
> *Oh Great Cyber Mother keep us whole*
> *Let your love and power fill our souls*
> *Oh Great Cyber Father keep us whole*
> *Let your love and power fill our souls.*
>
> *We are the flow, we are the ebb*
> *We are the weavers of the Wiccan Web.*
> *We are the flow, we are the ebb*
> *We are the weavers of the Wiccan Web.*
> *We are the flow, we are the ebb*

We are the weavers of the Wiccan Web.
We are the flow, we are the ebb
We are the weavers of the Wiccan Web.
We are one with all, and all one! Blessed be!

Hold the two paper clips in between your hands and merge with the Cyber Spirit for a few moments. Link the clips together and say:

May the power and blessing of this Cyber group
Bless and flow into these symbols of unity.
Ayea Kerridwen! Ayea Kernunnos!
Ayea, Ayea, Ayea
So be it!

CLOSING THE CIRCLE   Do any magical work you have intended for this time. Toast the gods and goddesses, feast, and play metaphysical games with your cyber group. One game you can play is called The Talking Wand. Each member of the chat room, one by one, takes a virtual wand (representing the powers of air) in his or her hand, and then merging with the wand, he or she types out whatever comes into his or her mind. You can pick up a pick up a pen or pencil and hold it while merging if you don't have a virtual wand. Better yet, use your Craft wand if you have one. When everyone merges deeply enough, this ritual game can open many perceptual windows. Lastly, say your Merry parts, exchange e-mail addresses and Web sites, sign off, thank the gods and goddesses, and release your Sacred Cyber Circle. Your ritual is complete.

POSTRITUAL ACTIVITIES   Keep the joined paper clips on your computer altar or desk as a symbol of your unity with other like-minded Web Wiccans. Anytime you are feeling alone or depressed, take the paper clips in your hands and hold them for a few minutes, remembering the connection you have with other Wiccans across the world. Be sure to e-mail or send a virtual greeting card to a few of your new cyber friends in the next week or two.

RITUAL OF FORGIVENESS AND PEACE

Do you ever wish you could get together with someone you've had a falling-out with and make things right between you? Or, better yet, meet for a forgiveness ritual where the past gets buried and you begin building the future? Sometimes the miles between you and this individual become a barrier to breach. That's where the Internet steps in with assistance.

NECESSARY COMPONENTS   Sage and cedar smudge, a piece of rose quartz, honeysuckle oil, a bowl of salt, and a pink candle.

INVOCATION AND OPENING   Draw your Sacred Cyber Circle and call the Cyber Wards. You will be typing the ritual to the person you are bridging the gap with (via an instant messenger–type service).

RITUAL BODY   Type the following words to your friend:

> *Now and forever we cast away*
> *All that holds us now at bay*
> *Great Cyber Goddess, now we pray*
> *That sweet forgiveness may come our way.*
>
> *Join me now and cast away*
> *All pain and hurt and disdain*
> *Great Cyber God, now we pray*
> *That lasting peace may come our way.*
>
> *Great Cyber Spirits now hear our plea*
> *Open our hearts so that we may see*
> *Bless us now, keep our spirits free*
> *Forever and a day, blessed be!*

CLOSING THE CIRCLE   Chat with your friend for a while and resolve any differences as best as you can, realizing that this is just the first step in moving the energy between the two of you in a more positive direction. Remember that we are all reflections of each other. We are One. When you are done, thank the goddesses and gods and release the circle.

POSTRITUAL ACTIVITIES   Sprinkle the salt outside your doorway while you visualize casting away all feelings of negativity and hostility toward the person. Keep the piece of rose quartz as a reminder of the ritual and as a talisman for peaceful feelings and thoughts. Be sure to send the person a virtual card the next day, telling them how much they mean to you and how much better you feel now that you have worked out your problems and differences.

COMPUTER WIZARDRY

Perhaps the most exciting part of Web Witching is the way it inspires creative adaptation. There's a computer wizard in each Wiccan, just waiting to escape, explore, and have a little fun in the process. The purpose of this chapter is to share some of the fruits of our personal explorations with you. The hope here is that you can use many as they stand or tweak them somewhat to fit your own situations, and that they will inspire many more ideas of your own.

Adapting Traditional Wiccan Creeds and Texts

Like any other group, Wiccans have some basic ideas and writings that shape our conversations and our rites. But what happens to those flowery phrases when we take them into an atmosphere filled with nuts and bolts? They suddenly seem a little out of place, and even maybe a bit outdated. So, let's update them! The following adaptations are intended to be playful and fun. No disrespect in any way is intended toward the original creeds.

The Web Wiccan Rede

Do as you will and spam none.

The Charge of the Cyber Goddess

Listen to the rhythmic hum of the Great Cyber Mother, who of new is called the Wiccan Web Creatrix, Cyber Woman, and by many other names. Whenever you have need of anything, once in the month, and better it be when the moon is full, you shall assemble before your computer altar and behold the wonders of Me, who is the Queen of Cyberspace. You shall be free from drudgery and mundane thought when you stand here. Rather, eat, drink, make music and love in My presence, for Mine is the ecstasy of magic, and Mine is joy both today and tomorrow. Mine is the secret that opens the files to youthful energy, and Mine is the surging electricity of life—the grail of unlimited knowledge, unlimited spirit. I give knowledge of the eternal and beyond death I give peace and reunion with the Ancestors and My Mainframe from which you came. Nor do I demand sacrifices, for I am the Mother of All Things and my love pours through your CPU, you, and out through the earth.

Hear the words of the Star Goddess, the dust of whose feet are the bytes of all heaven and whose body encircles the Core. I who Am the beauty of the blue screen, the smooth-running hard drive, the spark of an on button, and the mysteries of Web Witching. I call upon your soul to rise and come to Me, for I Am She who gives life where none before existed. Let My worship be through your systems and lives; all acts of networking bring Me pleasure. Let there be beauty, strength, power, compassion, honor, humility, and wisdom within you. And know that which you seek is always within and without, on hardware as on software, above and below, as it has been from the beginning and will be at the end of desire.

The Charge of the Cyber God

Listen to the rhythmic hum of the Great Cyber Father, who of new is called the Wiccan Web Creator, Cyber Man, and by many other Hyperlink codes. My law is harmony and interaction with all things. Mine is the secret code that opens the files of life and mine are the crystalline components made from the earth that is the tower of Kernunnos that is the eternal circle of rebirth. I give the knowledge of life everlasting, and beyond death I give the promise of regeneration and renewal. I am King of Cyberspace, the sacrifice, the Father of All Things, and my protection blankets the earth.

Hear the hum of the running Cyber God, the music of whose laughter stirs the networks and channels, and whose hard drive initializes the seasons. I who Am the Cyber Lord of Search and Find and the Power of Comm Central, the Best of the Web, and the Secret of the Power Source. I call upon all old computers and mainframes to shut down and come unto Me. For I Am the crystalline Cyber Soul of the earth and all its electronic beings. Through Me all things must be deleted and recycled, and with Me are reassembled, reconfigured, and reborn. Let My worship be in the World Wide Web that dials, hums, connects, and sings, for behold, all acts of Web surfing and magic are My rituals. Let there be acts of In and Out, Power On and Power Off, Save and Trash, Receive and Send, Upload and Download, together with harmony and curiosity within your Cyberspace adventures. For these too are part of the crystalline mysteries found within yourself, within Me, as all is one continuous feedback loop, where all beginnings have endings, and all endings have beginnings.

The Law of Threefold Return

Whatever you send out on the Web will return to you threefold, be it energy or e-mail!

The Law of Three or Law of Threefold Return acts as a guideline for all Web Witches. Working from the basic principle of cause and effect, the Threefold Law decrees that what you send out on the Internet, you get back—only three times as strong, so make it good!

Mind ye threefold law ye should,
Three times bad and three times good.
(From the modern version of the "The Wiccan Rede.")

Each of us needs to take responsibility for our Web Witching experiences and actions, as well as in everything we say, do, think, dream, and feel.

The Three-Finger Salute

In magical traditions, the moon is often honored in a salute that uses the thumb, pointer finger, and pinky held up to the lunar sphere. Adapting this, the Control, Alt, Delete function that reboots your computer becomes the cyber Three-Finger Salute. However, because this action causes a shift in power and transforms the screen, it might best be used in conjunction with solar-related efforts rather than lunar.

Computer Divination

There are several ways to use your system for divination. First, you can refer to online oracles, tarot, and astrology sites. The only caution here is to check the sites' credentials and references, and to shop around. It costs you nothing to look, and this will ensure that you find quality services at reasonable prices—or even for free!

Second, you can go to your local computer software store and check out astrology or biorhythm programs and so on. Just remember to have the information on your system's memory capacity and speed with you. This way you'll actually be able to *use* the software when you get home!

For those of you seeking a more hands-on approach, here are some rather fun and creative ways we've come up with to use your computer for divination.

Scrying

For the purpose of this exercise you'll want to leave your computer's screen blank (but you can power up the system to represent Spirit's flow through it). Sit in a comfortable chair in front of the screen. Close your eyes for a moment and take several deep, cleansing breaths. As you do, focus your intent on a question. Now, open your eyes and look at the screen. Don't look for anything specific; let your vision blur slightly.

With time and practice images will start appearing on the screen similar to those you might see in a crystal ball, and for many people the screen images are clearer and more literal. Why? Because we already expect the computer screen to reveal words and images to us in a literal form, and so our superconscious responds to that expectation. Even if you don't get highly obvious images, you can still interpret what you see as you would any result from a scrying sphere. Here's a brief interpretation guide to which you can refer:

Black patterns   A negative sign, especially if moving down or to the left. Also self-control issues.

Blue patterns   Joy and hope. The sky is clearing!

Brown patterns   Use practicality here. Ground yourself and move slowly.

Green patterns   News is forthcoming (refer to the color, movement, or patterns to know if it's good or bad news).

Gray patterns   Things about a certain situation are "iffy." Focus on developing yourself before doing anything else.

Orange patterns   Move confidently! Socialization and possible new relationships.

Pink patterns   Serving others will help you in achieving a goal.

Purple patterns   The need for introspection, especially with regard to spiritual matters. Heal yourself.

Red patterns   The need to assert yourself and speak honestly. Matters of faith.

White patterns   A good sign, especially if moving up or to the right.

Yellow patterns   Some type of surprise (the shade of yellow or pattern itself often indicates if the surprise will be good or bad).

To expand the potential interpretive value of your efforts, refer to a dream symbol key, or any divination book that provides the meanings of icons and symbols (try Trish's book *Futuretelling* from Crossing Press).

Net-o-Mancy

Think of something you'd like to know and find a keyword or phrase that corresponds to the core of your question. Focus on this intently as you type that word or phrase into your favorite search engine. Wait for the listings to come onto your screen.

Now, close your eyes, still focusing on the question. Randomly keystroke down to any entry that the search engine finds (hey, no peeking). Go to that site and see what messages Spirit has for you!

Automatic Typing

Think of a situation in which you need perspective or a question you'd like the answer to. Close your eyes and hold out the index finger of your strong hand. Purposefully press three random keys on your keyboard (again—no peeking), then see what set of letters, numbers, or symbols come up. Letters can represent the initials of a person, place, or thing; numbers can be interpreted according to numerology; and symbols add more dimension to the information you're getting. For example, an exclamation point would emphasize what the message says, a plus sign might indicate financial or personal gains, and a minus sign might indicate losses or decrease.

For those of you who have knowledge of how to safely commune with spirits, you can take this process a little further. In this case, rather than physically becoming a medium for the spirit, you can let that entity "borrow" your hands. Close your eyes and let words flow into them. Type until you feel done, and see what messages come from either the astral realm or your higher self in the process.

All Keyed Up

In chapter 3 we mentioned using loose keys from an old keyboard as a divination tool. Since the keys are all the same shape and size, you can make this into a drawn or cast system depending on your preference. In either case, you'll want a cloth bag to house the keys in. You'll also want to create a list of the keys bearing numbers, words, or emblems on them, and how to interpret them depending on where they fall in the reading.

Letters are pretty straightforward, often indicating initials, addresses, or even spelling whole words. Numbers can bear the same values as they do in numerology, with the minor variances that the symbols above them create. For example, since the 7 key bears the ampersand, it might represent something being finished just before another project or goal begins (as in an addition or inclusion).

Here are some ideas on how to interpret the other keys; however, we strongly recommend writing out your own system. It will help you memorize the symbolic values and give more meaning to the overall kit.

Backspace   Either you need to back off from a person or situation, or you're somehow digressing in the way you cope with life. Don't backslide! Keep on keepin' on!

Caps Lock   Stop shouting or projecting your energy so much. Whispers and self-control speak much more loudly to those you really want to reach.

Control   You are either exerting too much control in this situation or aren't being domineering enough. Don't micromanage yourself or companions to the point of tedium.

End   A conclusion and closure. Something is about to end naturally, or perhaps it's time to create an ending before matters get out of hand.

Equal   The need for balance or equity with a person, or in a specific situation. What the equal points to may make this particular key's meaning clearer.

Escape   What are you trying to run away from? Is it really time for a hasty retreat? This key councils us that we need to know when to stand our ground.

Home   Redirect your attention to your living space and the people within it who may have been neglected of late.

Insert   A change needs to occur in your life—something's missing
   here. Figure out what it is, and you'll see things improve greatly.
Num Lock   You're too caught up in logical thinking. Release
   yourself and your spirit, and begin listening to instincts and the
   small voice within.
Pause   Don't keep rushing forward. Stop for a moment and
   carefully consider your words or actions before proceeding.
   Alternatively, this may indicate someone in need of a vacation.
Shift   This may indicate some kind of transition, often in the way
   you think about or handle things. Try backing up a bit and
   getting some perspective.
Tab   Movement (forward or back).

Diagnostic Divination

For this you'll need a tiny computer screwdriver or other computer-related part or implement that can be easily tied to the end of
a string for pendulum work. Since your computer's system is based
on binary code, this particular form of divination is most successful
if you limit it to yes–no answers.

Hold the makeshift pendulum over the area of your computer
where the problem seems to originate (usually the tower). Wait for
it to become still and begin concentrating on simple questions (Is
this problem caused by software?). Movements forward and back-
ward indicate an affirmative response, while left to right movements
are negative.

When you get a "hit" (a yes movement), then go on to ask more
specific questions. For example, if the pendulum indicated a software problem, name each piece of software one at a time. The one
that comes up as a yes is the place to begin your diagnostic process.

Computer Pathworking

Each time you go online and begin to search the Internet you are
performing a kind of pathworking; each decision leads you some-

where specific, often resulting in your gaining knowledge. In this case we're going to take the process a little further and make it more purposeful. Before beginning, however, you should know that some online sites have pathworking exercises available. Check the sites of Order of Bards, Ovates and Druids, and any other sites dedicated to exploring mazes or labyrinths. Going to these sites will likely save you time, but may not yield the desired results.

In order to work on your personal cyber-path, you'll first want to get into a deeply meditative state of mind. Sit before your computer altar, get comfortable, light some candles, burn incense, and create a good atmosphere for introspection. Have a notebook and pen or a tape recorder handy. When you feel ready, go to your favorite search engine and type in the topic (a key theme or phrase) that the pathworking is intended to bring into focus.

Next, browse the listings that come up. If there are a lot, scan the list and let your senses guide you. When you feel you've found the right site, go to it. Read over the information given there and see how it changes your feelings or perspective. If the site has links, scan the links too. Choose one (this is like the divided path in the woods—you can only follow one). Take this process as far as possible. Trust Spirit and your inner voice for guidance. Or, if there are no links from which to create your pathworking web, return to the main search listings and look for another one that calls to you. Repeat the process.

Don't rush any steps along this journey—let everything you're finding sink in on a symbolic or literal level. Make notes of the things that really impress you, and how the decision to follow a particular listing resulted in awareness. For example, say you were doing a pathworking about power and one of the Web pages you surveyed had a graphic of firecrackers on the main page. This might represent a need to control your energy more so it doesn't reach critical mass.

Review your notes later on so you can internalize the lessons and even expand upon them.

Cyber Gods and Goddesses

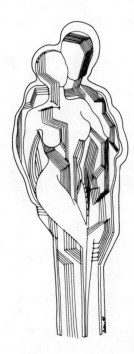

Throughout magical history we find practitioners around the world looking to the Divine to empower and bless their efforts. In designing your altar, creating sacred space, casting spells, or enacting rituals, you may wish to do likewise. But how do you choose suitable gods and goddesses for Web Witching?

Well, you can certainly look to divine beings who preside over any form of weaving, such as the Norns. You might also look to beings who are patrons or patronesses of the magical arts, since yesterday's magic has become today's technology! You could call upon a god or goddess from your magical tradition's pantheon, or one suited to the magic at hand. A lot here depends on your outlook.

Following is a list of gods, goddesses, and spirits who, by their attributes, can amplify and assist in your Web Witching efforts. Anytime you call upon a power such as one of these beings, please do so with respect. Make an effort to learn something about that deity, his or her culture, personality, legends, attributes, and how to correctly pronounce his or her name before invoking that presence into your sacred cyber space.

Remember, the goddesses and gods are your friends, guides, and protectors. They are always present to assist and help you in your Web Witching efforts, but in order to access their wisdom and power you need to call upon them with intent and love. Keep in mind that this is a two-way exchange: They seek to learn through you, just as you seek to learn from them.

Celtic

Angus mac Og   A god who can help heal glitches in your system, and help in Web romances and cyber courting rituals.

Aine   Irish earth and sun goddess to call upon when Web Witching on the Summer Solstice and Midsummer's Eve.

Airmed   A goddess who is especially helpful when searching and gathering information about herbs and herbal magic and healing.

Amaethon   The Harvest King who brings fruitfulness to your Web business ventures. Can assist in cultivating Web connections and plowing through vast amounts of information on the Internet.

Andraste   Web patroness of virtual sanctuaries.

Anu (Danu)   Great Mother of all cyber witches and the Wiccan Web.

Arawn   An ancestral god who can help during times of transition when upgrading to a new system and selling, giving away, or dismantling your old system. Assists in cyber shape-shifting adventures.

Arianrhod   Lunar and stellar goddess, keeper of the Silver Wheel. She is helpful when Web Witching at night, particularly on the Sabbats and Esbats.

Artio   The goddess of cyber bear shape-shifting adventures. Call upon her for power and courage.

Badb   A goddess who can neutralize Internet enemies and Web attacks. Hand those that send you spam over to her.

Banba   An Irish earth goddess to call upon when initiating your Web Witching adventures. She is particularly helpful when naming your site or computer.

Belenus   A sun god of light and healing who assists in Web healing rituals, spellworking, and surfing.

Belisama   A goddess of the rising sun to call upon while surfing in the early morning hours.

Belisana   A goddess of healing and laughter who assists in all Web projects that have to do with helping nature and the Earth.

Boann   A goddess of the river of information that flows on the Web. She aids those on the Web who help rivers stay alive and flowing.

Borvo   A patron god of the Web, of unseen and concealed truth, and inspiration through dreams.

Bran   A god protector of all creative artists on the Web.

Branwen   A Welsh love goddess who helps with cyber romances and love.

Bridget   The goddess of inspiration and communication. She is very helpful in all computer and Internet matters! Invoke her on Imbolc, and anytime you fire up your computer or turn on your printer.

Cliodna   A bird goddess who assists in cyber shapeshifting and delivering Web messages.

Cordemanon   Patron god of Web Witching. Associated with the Great Database of Knowledge.

Coventina   A goddess who helps in the creation (the birthing) of your Web page, domain, or Webring. Invoke her on the Spring Equinox.

Creidne   A metalworking god to call upon when selecting the most appropriate computer system.

Cu Chulainn   The Hound of Chulainn assists you in conquering any cyber challenges.

Dagda   A patron god of Web Witching, especially Web rituals and feasting. Invoke him on Samhain.

Dianacht   A god of cyber healing rituals.

Dumiatis   A god of creative surfing, Web stories, and learning magical skills from the Wiccan Web.

Eriu   The Triple Mother Goddess of Erin, who can help you with cyber shapeshifting and setting up and naming your page or domain.

Gobannon   A master craftsman god who can help you set up your system and keep it running smoothly.

Gwalchmei   A god to call upon when adding audio clips to your page or when surfing audio sites. Invoke him when sending virtual greeting cards that include sound.

Gwydion   A master god who assists you in any kind of cyber shapeshifting, magic, and eloquence.

Kernunnos   The Great Father God and lord of cyber power animals. Helps attract wealth through the Web.

Kerridwen   The goddess of all knowledge and wisdom on the Wiccan Web. Ask her to help you manifest your heart's desire from the Web.

Llyr   A sea god to call upon to make your computer system flow smoothly and your cyber efforts successful.

Luchta   A protector god who helps you shield your computer system from any negativity, including viruses.

Lugh   The master of all arts, including the cyber arts. A great protector and benefactor of all Web Witches. Invoke him on Lughnassad.

Mabon   "The Son of Light," who assists in cyber divination.

Manannan Mac Llyr   A teacher god to call upon when learning new skills over the Internet. He also helps with cyber shapeshifting efforts.

Math (Son of Mathonwy)   A Welsh teacher god to call upon when doing any kind of cyber magic and sorcery.

Medb   A powerful warrior queen and goddess who can be called upon when engaging in cyber sex magic and sensual surfing.

Mei   A goddess who helps keep your system grounded, your screen bright and clear, and your printer running smoothly.

Merlin (Myrddin)   One of the most excellent cyber companions and teachers of the nature of the Web.

Mider   The Faery king who is the best one to call upon when playing any kind of game on the Internet.

Morgana   The Death Mother who helps when you are getting rid of your old system. Also useful when ridding yourself of negative cyber connections and spam.

Morrigan   "The Phantom Queen" who can be used to cast off any negativity or dysfunctional components in your system. Invoke her on Samhain. Takes care of spam permanently.

Morrigu   The Dark Gray Lady who assists in retiring old systems and outdated software.

Nantosuelta   A river goddess who keeps your system running smoothly and the information flowing.

Nemetona   Great protectress of all computer systems, Internet connections, Web groups, and Webrings.

Nimue   An empowering goddess who holds the key to cyber magic and divination.

Nuada (of the Silver Hand)   A Celtic cyber god who aids in Web issues of leadership and hierarchy. Protects your computer from lightning and power surges.

Nwyvre   An excellent god for all Web surfing, especially when downloading new information.

Ogma   A master binder who can help you find the right words and sacred symbols. An ace communication and connection god!

Rhiannon   A Great Queen Goddess who assists in sending messages of any kind over the Web.

Rosemerta   A goddess who helps attract abundance to all your Web Witching business efforts.

Sinann   A river goddess who can make sure your Internet connection is strong and flowing.

Sirona   A goddess who is helpful when doing any kind of Web Witching and surfing.

Taliesin   He is particularly useful when engaging in any kind of creative arts in relation to the Web, especially music, poetry, and writing (including HTML code).

Triana The Triple Goddess—Sun-Ana, Earth-Ana, and Moon-Ana—who can help guide and protect you in all of your Web Witching experiences.

Viviana A goddess to call upon when setting up your system and hooking up to the Web.

Egyptian

Bast A cat goddess you can call upon to help you in cyber magic dealing with love. The ideal computer altar companion. One way to call Bast in is to invite your cat (every good Web Witch has one!) to sit on top of your computer monitor. Sirona's cat has done this since she was a kitten. When she's up there Sirona has noticed that her surfing and Web Witching efforts are much more pleasant and successful.

Hathor A goddess of love (called the Mother of Creation) who can help you expand your awareness in all of your Web Witching and surfing efforts.

Heket A frog goddess who assists in creating Web pages, sites, and links. Candles in shapes of frogs and other animals are ways to access her energy on your computer altar.

Horus The perfect god to call upon for help in troubleshooting your computer system.

Isis Web Witch extraordinaire! A goddess to whom weaving is sacred, she also assists in getting good computer advice when needed.

Khnum A god to call upon when creating your Web page and when creating links to your site.

Meskhenet A goddess of Web page and domain creation.

Min A god for fruitful and productive Web Witching and partnerships.

Nephthys A goddess of cyber divination and hidden knowledge that can be discovered on the Web.

Osiris   The Father God of civilization and rebirth, perfect to call upon when disassembling your computer or adding components. Also an excellent patron god of new systems.

Greco-Roman

Adonis   A Greek god who can help you find beauty and love over the Wiccan Web.

Apollo   A Greek god of accomplishment upon whom you can call to help you learn the art of Web Witching and Web divination. One of Apollo's sacred animals was a mouse!

Aphrodite   A Greek goddess of love, pleasure, and beauty who can assist in cyber relationships.

Artemis   Greek moon Web Witching goddess.

Cronus   The Greek god of time. Call on him to help when your computer's clock gets misconfigured.

Cupid   A Roman god of love and an essential helper when Web Witching for love and romance!

Dactyls   Spirits who invented magical formulae, and who were originally formed from Rhea's fingerprints. Call upon them to help with keyboard-related matters or when working on a programming issue.

Demeter   A goddess of fertility and prosperity who can be called upon to help when creating a Web business or partnership.

Dionysus   The god of feasting, ecstasy, and pleasure; he is especially helpful when doing rituals and Web Witching for pleasure.

Eros   A god who assists in Web Witching affairs of the heart.

Flora   A Roman goddess helpful in spring surfing, rituals, and spellworking. Real or virtual flowers honor this lady. Invoke her when sending virtual greeting cards!

Fortuna   The Roman goddess of luck, helpful in creating fortunate Web Witching experiences.

Graces   The three Greek goddesses of love, dancing, and gentleness, particularly useful in chat rooms and online rituals.

Graiae   All-seeing spirits who can assist with cyber scrying efforts.

Hecate   The patroness of witches and avid supporter of spellcraft. One of Hecate's symbols is a key, so if you have a lock on your computer system, you can dedicate it (and the associated key) to her!

Helen   Greek moon goddess who can be called upon when creating your Web page or when upgrading your site or domain.

Hera   A Greek goddess who helps in Web handfastings.

Hermes   Great for Internet messaging, sending and receiving e-mail, help in chat rooms, and keeping the Web lines open.

Hephaestus   The Greek god of metalsmithy who can assist the smooth operation of any metallic portion of your system.

Janus   A Roman god who is an excellent guide for navigating the Web.

Juno   A Roman goddess who is helpful in any kind of Web Witching that requires communication and messages or joining of users. The e-mail goddess!

Logos   The Greek god of reason who can help you with any of your computer's logical functions.

Pan   A god of cyber rituals and celebrations, also a patron god of sex magic and sensual surfing adventures.

Penelope   A Greek spring goddess of fertile Web connections and creation. Invoke her on the Spring Equinox.

Psyche   A goddess of romantic Web Witching adventures.

Selene   A moon Web Witching goddess.

Venus   A Roman love goddess who assists in Web Witching affairs of the heart.

Vulcan   Call upon this god when you "fire up" your computer.

Eastern Religions

Agni   A mediator god who can help us communicate more effectively with the spirit of our computer (his emblems include a fan and fire).

Akupera A goddess to help you with cyber moon magic.

Annapurna A Great Mother Goddess of plenty who can help you in your cyber adventures.

Ayizan A goddess to bless your first attempt at Web Witching with your system (initiation) or when you're surfing for goods and services (goddess of the marketplace).

Bhaga A god of fortune and prosperity who assists with financial Web concerns.

Chandra A god of fertility who is helpful during moon Web Witching.

Ganesha A god who removes obstacles. Call upon him to help break down communication barriers on the Net, or whenever you encounter deterrents to Web Witching efforts.

Kama (Kamadeva) Called the "Seed of Desire," he is an excellent patron god for Web romances, relationships, and sensual surfing!

Krishna A Hindu god who is helpful in all Web Witching efforts. Invoke him to get chats going strong!

Kwan Yin A goddess who assists in keeping surfing harmonious and Web Witching connections peaceful and loving.

Lakshmi A Hindu goddess for fortunate Web Witching.

Lalita A Hindu tantric goddess to consult in matters of cyber sex magic.

Maya A perfect cyber goddess of Web page and domain creation, any kind of surfing, and mother of the illusive Wiccan Web.

Mayavati/Rati A Hindu goddess who can be called on for some passionate Web Witching and surfing.

Mitra A Hindu god of cyber friendships and connections, great in chat rooms!

Parvati A Hindu goddess of Web romances and handfastings.

Pratisamvit A goddess of logic who can assist with your computer's analytical functions.

Radha A Hindu goddess to call upon when pursuing Web romance and love.

Sarasvati   The god who governs the keyboard (considered the creator of Sanskrit).

Shakti   The Great Hindu Mother Goddess who embodies feminine energy everywhere, including the Web.

Shiva   A Hindu god of creation who embodies masculine energy everywhere, including the Web.

Norse and Teutonic

Bragi   A god of cunning, artifice, and effective communication, Bragi helps with networking.

Frey   Call on this god for joyful and happy surfing adventures or when chatting in a chat room for the first time.

Freya   A goddess of love who can assist in Web romances.

Frigga   A goddess of the Web Witching feminine arts, with a fondness for hawks and falcons (real and virtual)!

Fulla   A goddess for fruitful Web Witching. Thank her when your disks are full from downloading information from the Web.

Gerda   A goddess of beauty and light who can assist you in setting up your computer altar and keeping it booted up.

Lofn   A Scandinavian love goddess who smooths over problems in Web Witching relationships and partnerships.

Norns   The three fates in whose hands a person's destiny is created. Call upon them for assistance in networking and divination. Excellent helpers for creating your Web site.

Odin   The chief god of this pantheon to whom runes are sacred. Call on Odin by writing your computer's name in runes and taping it to your tower. Invoke Odin to help create unique fonts or whenever you're working with magical scripts and names. The master of words and their power.

Thor   A thunder god who can protect your system from lightning, power disruptions, and power-supply problems. Use the symbol of the thunderbolt to invoke him.

Var   A Scandinavian love goddess who watches over Web
romances.

Others

Abtagigi   A Sumerian goddess of cyber sex magic.

Astarte   Great Assyro-Babylonian Mother Goddess who is
especially helpful for Web Witching during those times when
Venus appears in the sky.

Bel/Baal   Assyro-Babylonian sky god and patron god of Web ·
Witching and the expanding Web Circle.

Chango   A great African love god and king who is the patron of
cyber drum circles as well as any concerns of the heart over the
Internet.

Ishtar   A Babylonian goddess associated with the morning star.
She is particularly helpful when Web Witching or surfing in the
early morning hours.

Isong   An African goddess of sensual surfing adventures.

Kusor   A Phoenician god of magical formulas who can help with
writing HTML code or customized programming (and any
"cursor" problems).

Oshun   An African goddess to call upon in Web Witching matters
of love.

6

REACH OUT
AND TOUCH SOMEONE

Since this book is all about Web Witching and networking with like-minded folks, this chapter will provide you with more magical helps and hints to make your surfing time fulfilling and fun. The focus of this chapter is communicating with other pagans on the Wiccan Web in creative, intelligent, compassionate, and magical ways.

Wiccan Web Netiquette

When you log on to the Wiccan Web, you are entering a culture with its own social framework. There are generally accepted guidelines that most Web Witches use when surfing the Wiccan Web.

There's nothing worse than running into rude and mean people, even if it's remotely. So, to make sure everyone gets along, certain codes of conduct have been established by users around the world. Netiquette (or Network Etiquette) is a set of guidelines for online behavior. We have adapted the basic netiquette concepts for Web Witches.

The Wiccan Web often brings together people who probably would never have met otherwise. Unfortunately, the impersonality of cyberspace often changes normally kind humans into cyber morons. Even though most practitioners of the Craft don't dabble in negativity, there are still a few folks that just don't get the concept of Oneness and use the Wiccan Web to perpetuate their negativity.

Many of us have been victims of negative e-mail attacks. However, you don't have to put up with it. Contact the offender's Internet Service Provider (ISP). (You can figure out who the attacker's ISP is by looking at the text after the @ sign in the perpetrator's e-mail address; for example, in the address moron@aol.com, the ISP is aol.com.) Sometimes a service provider will terminate an offender's contract as a punishment for offensive behavior or sending out spam from a noncommercial e-mail address.

If you feel you must respond to negative e-mail you receive, do so by letting the sender know that you will be reporting him or her to the service provider. Remind the sender that all Internet activity is retrievable and that he or she is ultimately responsible for his or her own actions.

Thirteen-Point Wiccan Web Netiquette Checklist

1. *Remember that there are other humans out there when you are in cyberspace.* Treat others as you would like them to treat you. It's important to honor the opinions of others, but you don't necessarily need to embrace them. Be polite and don't become abusive when interacting with others. Avoid hurting people's feelings whenever possible, but express and stand up for yourself and your ideas. Ask yourself, "Would I say this to this person's face?" If the answer is no, change your words until you know that you would feel as comfortable saying the words to the live person as you would sending them on the Wiccan Web. Keep in mind that misinterpreting e-mail, chat comments, and other information on the Web is easy to do, so always ask for clarification whenever possible to avoid sticky cyber situations.

2. *Use the Wiccan Web to explore new cyber worlds, to express yourself, and to electronically travel where you've never gone before.* Cyber travel is the next best thing to being there. Check out sites in other countries and see what's happening in Craft circles all across the world. Participate in chat rooms with druids in England, or surf to a solitary practitioner's Web page in Norway. Most foreign sites have English translations available.

3. *Keep your nose clean and keep your Web activity legal.* Try to adhere to the same standards of behavior online as you do offline. Because of the impersonal quality of the Web, some people think it's okay to have a separate set of electronic ethics. Obviously standards of behavior are different in some areas of cyberspace, but it is still important to always be ethical when surfing, chatting, e-mailing, doing rituals, while in clubs, or when you are engaged anywhere else on the Web. As you know, ethics are a matter of personal choice, but be careful not to fool yourself into thinking that the correct choice of behavior on the Web is anything you can get away with. Remember, all exchanges of information are backed up and can be retrieved by your provider. Also, any messages that mention or support illegal activities may be reported by your provider to the authorities. Even though we are way past 1984, don't kid yourself—Big Brother is still watching you, and the Internet has made it a lot easier for him!

4. *Carry on the Wiccan Web tradition of contributing to world knowledge by sharing expert and reliable information about things like rituals and spells.* After all, the Internet was founded by people who wanted to share information. Now we can all carry the cyber scepter by daring to share what we know about the Craft. This is particularly useful to many members of the pagan communities because for many years most traditions only shared their knowledge with initiates of their own path. Now with the advent of the Wiccan Web, much of this secret knowledge is being uploaded on to the Internet, so you can get a copy for yourself. Given time, perhaps all traditions will have Web sites with their Books of Shadows, spells, rituals, and other information posted right there where everyone can read, download, adapt, and apply it.

Many Web Witches are posting lists of FAQs (frequently asked questions), resource lists, bibliographies, and useful pagan links, helping to make the Wiccan Web a more exciting place in which to chat and surf. When posting information you'd like others to have access to, be sure to give your name (Craft or otherwise), contact information, and to state in writing whether or not your writing is copyrighted.

5. *Remember that the strength of the Wiccan Web is in numbers.* Reach out and connect with more like-minded pagans every day. There are several newsletters you can have automatically e-mailed to you, as well as pagan chat groups and classes that meet on a regular basis. The Web is an enormous electronic network, made up of millions of people, with the Wiccan population gathering together in cyber circles all over the world in great numbers. It is a very powerful tool for pagans, a tool that can be used to connect Wiccans together, to organize and create greater awareness in the public eye as to what Wicca and the Craft are really about. The incredible thing about the Wiccan Web is it is essentially a worldwide circle of pagans who are loosely connected together into one enormous cyber spirit. This spirit can serve as an element for positive change in the future of humankind and our planet.

6. *Locate yourself in cyberspace.* Netiquette varies from site to site, chat room to chat room, so it's vital that you know just where you are on the Wiccan Web. When you enter a new domain in cyberspace such as a pagan chat room, spend a few minutes listening to (reading) the chat. Get an idea of the topic and who is in the room. After you get an overview of what's going on, go ahead and participate if it's your bag. If not, surf to another site that better suits you.

7. *Be a well-informed Web Witch.* Nothing is more of a turn off than having to navigate through a lot of misinformation, especially when it doesn't make any sense. Unfortunately, a lot of incorrect and incomplete information exists on the Web, which is why it is crucial to consider the source. Question everything, especially authority! Always check your facts, using other sources such as books, magazines, reliable Internet sites, or by checking with experts

in the subject area. Just about everyone who is an expert in any given field can be reached on the Internet. This is particularly true of pagan authors, teachers, groups, and other practitioners. Both of us welcome e-mail questions from readers, and we always try to respond promptly.

8. *Spend a little time developing your online image.* Make a good impression. People can't see you, so the color of your eyes, hair, and skin don't figure into the picture. You won't be judged by your body shape, how you smell, your age, the price tags on your clothing, or the car you drive. Your magical skill, the quality of your communication, the nuts and bolts of your writing, the words you choose and the way you use them are the factors others use to relate to you on the Wiccan Web. Remember, since the Web is mostly verbally driven, spelling and grammar *do* count. Use your Spell Check whenever possible. The graphics, fonts, layouts, and audio files you select for your Web page and the chat images and emoticons you use all reflect your online image.

9. *Have respect for Web Witching privacy.* Don't read other people's e-mail, and don't forward e-mail to others that has been written for your eyes only. Sending and receiving personal e-mail is between you and your correspondent. If you think someone is reading your e-mail, one thing you can do is plant false information in the messages and see if the culprit mentions or asks you about what you have planted. Keep in mind that in reality, e-mail is not private or secure because your provider has access to all of your messages. Hacking into someone else's Web page, besides being a criminal action, is also considered a BIG Web faux pas.

10. *Keep time in perspective.* Everyone seems to have less time available today than yesterday. Because there is so much information to digest these days, think twice before you send people copies of e-mail you have received. Think about whether the recipient will really appreciate that joke/survey/chain letter that's been floating around. Every time you send a message, you are taking up someone else's time. In addition, give people time to respond to e-mails you've sent, and understand that some people won't respond at all.

Also, when using newsgroups, don't post repetitive messages or messages that are off the topic of the message board. This generally annoys everyone—not just Web Witches.

11. *Forgive minor infractions of netiquette by Wiccan Web rookies and cut everyone a little slack for making mistakes.* Not everyone has had the benefit of reading this book, so allow for things like stupid questions, misspellings, and long-winded answers. Give Web Witches the benefit of the doubt, ignore minor errors, and take a few deep breaths before responding rather than immediately reacting to Internet blunders. It's always better to respond *politely* by private e-mail rather than publicly posting a scathing remark.

12. *Flaming, usually in response to obvious flame bait, is a long-standing network tradition.* Flaming is when you express your opinion without holding anything back, and is generally done in public chat rooms or on Web forums. If done correctly, flaming can be exciting and loads of fun, especially if the recipient of the flame deserves the hot seat! What isn't cool is perpetuating flame wars on the Wiccan Web. These kind of wars, usually among a handful of people, often dominate the tone of a chat and can destroy the cohesion of a discussion group. Flame wars are a senseless monopolization of the Wiccan Web.

13. *Tailor your language to fit the cyberspace you're in.* The pros and cons of swearing on the Web have been tossed back and forth by just about everyone. Whether of not you swear on the Web is your business, but keep in mind it is not allowed on certain sites, and chat rooms that are open to children, for example. Some people are offended by swearing and others are not, so be mindful of who you are communicating with. Also, search engines will often have you list your site in the "adult" listings if there are swear words in it. You can always use the classic asterisk and symbol filler, for example, f!*k it. Most everyone will still know exactly what you mean. A rule of thumb is to avoid offending anyone needlessly. As Buckaroo Bonzai said, "Don't be mean, don't be mean. Remember no matter where you go, there you are." That applies to cyberspace as well as ordinary reality.

Web Circle Netiquette

The essence of the Wiccan Web is diversity; however, because of this we cannot always assume that everyone shares the same ideas about what is acceptable behavior in a ritual space. One thing each of us can do is to extend the same respect to others that you desire from them. Following is a list of cyber circle pointers that you can tailor to your needs and tradition.

1. *A cyber ritual is a spiritual ceremony*, and one in which considerable energy can be raised and directed in specific ways. Participants need to be careful and, ideally, in a magical state of awareness.

2. *Cyber ritual space is sacred space*, just like your cyber altar. Please don't defile the Wiccan Web! Cyber sacred space is consecrated space.

3. *Within cyber ritual circles each participant should be treated with respect*, no matter who they are. Make an effort to stay in the perfect love, perfect peace, perfect trust mode while participating in a Cyber Circle.

4. *Never threaten another Web Witch's well-being, especially in a Cyber Circle.* Instead, make an effort to keep the Wiccan Web strong, flexible, and healthy.

5. *If you don't want to participate*, exit and go to another Cyber Circle or surf the Web.

6. *Don't waste the time of the people that are already in the Cyber Circle wih a lot of idle gossip and banter.* Instead use chat or e-mail.

7. *Be fully conscious of what is going on in the Circle and your role in it.* Remember, rituals and chats are often posted to the Web so everyone can read them.

8. *Be prepared if you are leading the ritual.* Know what your part is in the ritual body itself.

9. *Merge with the energies of the Cyber Circle* and check in to see or sense how you can join in the ritual in order to contribute toward the build-up of magical energies. Participate in the ritual, don't just sit there spectating!

10. *If you are late to a ritual that is already in progress*, be prepared to wait outside of the Cyber Circle, without causing distraction. Then get in on the postritual activities and chat.

11. *Once the Cyber Circle has been cast, enter or leave only when you absolutely need to*, and when you do, go through the Little Cyber Gate, closing it behind you.

12. *When the ritual is complete*, check to see if there is some sort of contribution you can make toward the next ritual. Helping out benefits you as well as all others. After all, within the Wiccan Web, we are woven into One.

Dos and Don'ts for Internet Neopagans and Wiccans

For those of you who are newer computer users, this section will give you some solid dos and don't about the Internet. Some of these hints may seem like common sense, and others may appear overly cautious, but remember two things as you read this section. First, practical magic does not forego logic and rational thinking; it uses both as helpmates. Second, the world is not always as kind and honest as we might wish it to be. The Internet provides an excellent mask for scams and ill-motivated individuals to hide behind, so our cautions here are not without foundation. Any tool, including the Internet, can be used for boon or bane; our intention is to help you use it for the greatest good and as a magical aid that will benefit you spiritually and temporally every day.

Don'ts

Don't expect search engines on the Internet to be organized or efficient. They're not. It takes a while to get really good at using effective search words and knowing which sites to chose once the search engine has returned the listings. Use your Rite of Web Witching to help with this.

Don't expect that people are all that they seem on the Internet. Even if someone says he or she is *neo-pagan*, even if you get a photograph of a home altar, be aware that anyone can scan *any* photograph and e-mail it to someone saying it's of something personal. The Internet is, in many ways, quite impersonal, and you will need to rely on your magical/psychic instincts quite a lot.

Don't ever give out your address or phone number to people you don't know. This is *especially* important for teens, lone elders, and young women who may go looking for a group to join, and find something not so pleasant.

Don't give out your birthdate, social security number, or other personal information unless you're using a secure server. Likewise, if you are buying goods online and choose to use a credit card, find a secure server that protects your personal information (a good example of a secure server is the service available through amazon.com).

Don't post flamebait! It's a very underhanded and manipulative practice, especially when done by skilled Web Witches.

Don't give out your password to anyone!

Don't abuse your power. Some individuals have more power than others in cyberspace (system administrators and Webmasters for example). Knowing more or having more "cyber power" than people does not give one license to take advantage of others. There's nothing more repugnant (or more disconnected) than an arrogant, self-righteous Web Witch!

Dos

Do get yourself a good antivirus program that will regularly scan your system for bugs. The most common causes of drive failure are viruses downloaded from Internet files and e-mail, even those that come from well-meaning magical friends. Be sure to scan all floppy disks with your antivirus software before opening them and *never* put a disk in the drive before you start your computer!

Do get yourself a good utility program like one of the ones made by Norton. This will help keep your system clean and in peak operational form, as you would want of any good magical tool.

Do ask your spiritual friends, family, and people you respect for the Web addresses of sites they frequent, especially ones with good links.

You'll probably be most pleased with these sites, or at the very least find others close to what you were looking for through them.

Do treat your computer with the same respect as any magical implement. Cleanse it with sage smoke regularly, bless it, and put other significant tokens around the area to augment the sacred space you're creating.

Do ask your favorite deities to guide and direct your efforts whenever you're surfing, and then really listen to your inner voice. This will help you locate the best sites for the subject at hand.

Do make an effort to keep private conversations private by using e-mail or private chat rooms and not message boards and announcement areas.

Do apply the Wiccan concepts of perfect love, perfect peace, and perfect trust in your cyber relationships, associations, and interactions, just as you do in your everyday life.

Internet Speak

When you communicate electronically, all you see is a computer screen. You don't have the opportunity to use facial expressions, gestures, and tone of voice to communicate your meaning; words are all you've got. And that goes for the person on the other end of the connection as well. On top of that, you can't see or sense how the other person is reacting to your words, graphics, Web symbols, audio files, and content.

Since many of the body signals that tell us about a person's attitude and feelings are missing in a text-based environment, you need to learn to signal textually and graphically what you would normally signal through your body language and tone of voice. This is where Internet Speak, acronyms, and emoticons come into the Wiccan Web picture.

Acronyms

The expanded use of the keyboard has become standard operating procedure for most Web Witches. The result is what looks like some sort of code or foreign language, with weird symbols and abbreviations. For your reference, we have put together a list of acronyms (abbreviations) and emoticons (symbols) most commonly used on the Web. You will find that by using acronyms, emoticons, and other symbols to express yourself, you will get more out of chats and other kinds of discussion groups.

Listed below are some common acronyms.

BRB   be right back
BTW   by the way
LOL   laugh out loud (lots of laughs)
ROFL   rolling on the floor laughing
IMO   in my opinion
IMHO   in my humble opinion
IYO   in your opinion
RL   real life
IRL   in real life
WRT   with regards to
TIA   thanks in advance
FWIW   for what it's worth
FYI   for your information
WYSIWYG   what you see is what you get (wizzywig)
RTFM   read the f!@#ing manual (flamebait)
TFN   thanks for nothing (flamebait)

Emoticons

Emoticons are a figure created with the symbols on the keyboard, usually read with the head tilted to the left. Look at the symbol sideways, with the colon on the top and the parentheses on the bottom and it's easy see what they symbolize. Emoticons are used to convey the spirit in which a line of text is typed.

Emoticons can clarify your words. For example, That was just great :-) (said with a smile) or That was just great :-((said with a frown). Use emoticons sparingly. Learn to infuse your conversation with occasional emotional cues. Some of these cues can be as simple as be an expression or body gesture typed between < > or ::. For example :: moving across the room to grab my chalice of wine:: Below is a list of Internet emoticons.

0:-)	What an angel!
:-)	Smile
:-)))	Really big smile
:-))))))))	Really, really big smile
:)	Funny, humor
:-):-(	Masks (theatrical comments)
:<)	A person with a moustache
:3)	A man with a handlebar moustache
:(	Frown
:<)=	For those with beards
:/)	Not funny
'-)	Wink
P-)	Pirate
;-)	Wink 2
(@@)	You're kidding!
:-"	Pursing lips
:-v	Another face (speaking), side profile
:-V	Another face (shouting), side profile
:-w	Speak with forked tongue
:-W	Shout with forked tongue
:-r	Sticking your tongue out
:-,	Smirk
<:-O	Eeek!
:-*	Oops! (covering mouth with hand)
:x	I'm not talking
:-T	Keeping a straight face (tight-lipped)
:-D	Said with a smile
:-O	More shouting
:-{	Count Dracula
=|:-)=	Uncle Sam
7:)	Cowboy

:-#	Censored
:~i	Smoking
:Q	Smoking II
:~j	Smoking and smiling
:/i	No smoking
:-I	It's something, but I don't know what
:-)x	Kiss
:-)xx	Two kisses
:-)~~~	French kiss
:-xo	A kiss and hug
:->	Another happy face
:-(	Unhappy
:-c	Really unhappy
:-C	No way! unbelieving (jaw dropped)
:-<	Forlorn
:-B	Drooling (or overbite)
:-|	Disgusted
:/	Cry
:D	Laugh
x-)	Confused
X-)	Really Confused
:-?	Licking your lips
<:>==	A turkey
:-):-):-)	A loud guffaw
:-J	Tongue-in-cheek comments
:*)	Clowning around
:-8	Talking out of both sides of your mouth
(:-)	Wearing a bicycle helmet
@=	Warning about nuclear war
<:-)	Asking dumb questions
o=	A burning candle
-=	A doused candle
OO	Headlights on a message
:_)	Nose out of joint
B)	Batman

B-|	Michael Keaton's Batman
#:-)	Someone with matted hair
&:-)	Someone with curly hair
=:-)	Someone with Bart Simpson hair
:-o	"Oh, nooooo!" (a la Mr. Bill)
|-(	Late night messages
:-{#}	Have braces
(:-&	Angry
:-	Angry II
(:-(	Very sad
(:<)	Blabbermouth
:-(=)	Buck teeth
@:-)	Wavy hair
?-(	Black eye
:	Messages about fuzzy things
8-)	Wears glasses
%-)	Broken glasses
+<:=|	Monk/nun
(O-)	Cyclops
(:-|K-	Formal message
||*(	Handshake offered
||*)	Handshake accepted
<&&>	Rubber chickens
><><	Argyle socks
2B|^2B	Message about Shakespeare
(-_-)	Smile
<{:-)}	Message in a bottle
<:-)<<|	Message from a space rocket
(:-...	Heartbreaking message
<<<<(:-)	A hat salesperson
(O_<	A fishy message
(:>-<	Message from a thief: hands up!
@—>——	A rose
{{{name}}}	Cyber hug

Wicca Speak

Since the Internet is filled with iconic shorthand languages and people are coming up with new emoticons all of the time, we thought it would be fun to create acronyms and emoticons specifically useful to Wiccans and many other members of the neopagan community. We call it Wicca Speak. Some of the Wicca Speak emoticons are meant to be looked at turned sideways like regular Internet emoticons, but not all of them. After all, witches like to be different. The first time you use these symbols in an e-mail, ICQ, or chat you may have to explain their meanings, but after that more and more people will pick Wicca Speak and use it! We encourage you to make up more and adapt the ones that are listed below.

Wicca Speak Acronyms

AWW   advanced Web Witch
A!   Ayea!
BWW   beginning Web Witch
BM   black moon
BB!   blessed be!
BAC   born-again Christian
CYCIR   cyber circle
CYRIT   cyber ritual
D1, D2, D3 . . .   Degrees, magical
FM   full moon
HP   High Priest
HPS   High Priestess
IWW   intermediate Web Witch
MC   Master of the Craft
MM   merry meet
MMA   merry meet again
MP   merry part
PL   perfect love
PP   perfect peace

PT   perfect trust
PPAG   practicing pagan (hoping to get it right)
SBI!   So be it!
SMB!   So mote it be!
WW   Web Witch
WWb   Wiccan wannabe
WWEB   Wiccan Web

Wicca Speak Emoticons

{} (like an open mouth)	Air element
*<———-	Activating your athame
~~><	Banishing negativity
o===	Candle burning
X===	Candle snuffed out
^	Cone of power
:o:	Coven or magic circle
:o:<——- :-)	Drawing the circle
:-) D—	Drinking from the chalice
Y—- :-)	Dousing
^^^	Earth element
\	God
*	Goddess (mother aspect)
888—888—888—	A grove (of trees)
@	Earth (where we are at)
[]!	Elder of the Craft
~~	Energy (the flow)
()	Fire element
##—-	Flyswatter
[G	Group intitated witch
|||	Group practitioner
%	Higher self vs. lower self
S—D :-)	Burning incense
8	Infinity
8:-)	Infinite mind

[	Initiate
[#	Initiation
——>.<——	Karmic kickback
oxxo#	Love magic
#	Magic (weaving patterns)
*!:-)	Manifestation
:-)\@*(-:	Merging with the God/Goddess
:-)&(-:	Merging together
(-)	Negative energy
(=)	Neutral energy
:(0):	Oneness
==	Parallel worlds
(+)	Positive energy
$#	Prosperity magic
Y	Protection
{?}	Questionable statement
-=+	Ritual (joining of energies)
[S	Self-initiated witch
:-)*#\(-:	Sex magic
|	Solitary practitioner
0	Spirit/source
S.....	Standing stones
3x3x3	Threefold law
D—- :-)	Toasting the Goddess/God
\\\	Triple God
)0(	Triple Goddess (or moon phases)
D—>—-	A tulip
X	Unity/harmony
]*/[	Universe (or yin/yang)
:-)*———-	Wand zapping energy to you
(	Waning Moon
)	Waxing Moon
'" (like raindrops)	Water element
*———:-)	Waving your magic wand
W:o:W	Wiccan Webring

Internet Chat Rooms

Chatting is truly a revolution of computer interactivity, and is a great way to meet other Web Witches on the Wiccan Web at a fraction of the cost of a long-distance phone call. Chatting is an immediate, cost effective way to discuss current topics of interest with other Web Witches and to share magical knowledge. An Internet chat allows you to exchange typed-in messages with others in an online environment called a chat room. Chat rooms can be found all over the Web; some are hosted by bulletin board services, Internet service providers, and Web sites.

Some chat rooms are always open and ongoing such as those at Talk City and America Online; others are scheduled for a certain time and date, such as neopagan.com, and often have a particular Sabbat or Esbat ritual or chat topic. Some chats have guest authors, experts, and famous people who are willing to chat with anyone who joins in. (Trish and Sirona often do public chats.) Transcripts of the chat are often archived and can be or called up if you want to read them over later. This is an excellent metaphysical exercise for gaining greater personal awareness. Oftentimes when you are in the midst of a chat, you may miss something that has been said, or you misunderstand something that is said, or you don't remember typing in certain comments.

The site hosting the chat room will often have free software for you to download that will enable you to participate in chats on that particular site. It's best to have a Java-enabled browser. When you go to a chat room site, a window will often appear on the screen, asking you if you want to download special software or, if you have the software, if you want to enable it.

Sometimes you need to be a registered member of the hosting Web site in order to chat. If you're not a registered member, you can often log in as a chat guest, and then register as a member later if the chat room is a place to which you'd like to return. Membership is often free—registration is just a way for the Webmaster at the site to keep a record of who is using the chat rooms. This brings us to the next point: Remember—everything you type in is being recorded, so think before you chat! Big Brother is still watching you. Your words are being stored for Web Witches (and anyone else) all over the world to read. Also consider the possibility that a few of our celestial neighbors even have their own way (the Web provider in the stars) of accessing the Web and are reading the chat too! Sometimes chat rooms take a few moments to load. Once they are loaded, you are ready to chat. Most of the time, there is a box on the chat screen in which you can type your comments. Once you press enter, your comment will be placed in the room for everyone to read. At the top of most chat screens, there are navigation bars with various links to other chat rooms and to other sites. You can always visit other chat rooms and surf to find the one most suited to your interests.

How to Enter Chat Rooms

Consider what name you want to be known by and use it consistently in that particular chat room. Trish always uses her real name (it's easier than remembering tons of pseudonyms). But for those who prefer their privacy, choosing a special magical "handle" for chat rooms (or for participating in a circle) is perfectly acceptable. Sirona uses several different chat names and likes to check in and see what folks are talking about using several other personas. Have fun, be creative, and choose a name that you really like, one that matches your goals for Web Witching, or use special magical names in certain chat rooms to help manifest the energy you desire.

Some chat sites such as Worlds Chat or the Palace (as well as 3D or virtual games sites) give you the option of using a graphic representation of yourself (called an avatar) in a virtual environment. In magic, an *avatar* is an incarnation of a deity, and is symbolic of your magical or higher self. Online, your avatar can be an eagle, unicorn, tiger, ET, or whatever kind of creature or object seems right to you. There are many images available for you to choose from.

Chat Room Netiquette

Most chat rooms have a basic set of rules that apply to the conduct in that room. Be sure you review them before you begin. Many chat rooms are not moderated, which means no one is keeping tabs on your conversation or censoring the room. Regardless, you'll still want to remain civil and to treat others as you'd like to be treated. If you want to interject a new idea or magical theme, ask if it's okay with everyone in the chat room, then wait your turn. Also, don't let yourself get sucked into witch bitch-sessions, wars, or conflicting group dynamics. This isn't the place to air dirty laundry or "dis" someone, and such discussions should be gently steered in a different direction, avoided, or directly stopped by confronting the "mad chatter." One nice thing about chats is you don't have to answer questions if you don't want to. Remember, if someone is rude or harasses you in a chat room, you can report the user to the host of the chat room, which may result in the offender being banned from that room. Of course, he or she may come back under another name and repeat the same mad chatter pattern, but be persistent. We've found that most everyone who chats on pagan sites and in Wiccan chat rooms is there to meet people, learn more about the Craft, and have fun. Also, whenever someone is being rude to someone else during a chat, the other Web Witches apply peer pressure and automatically shut the offender down. Humor also helps keep the lid on mad chatters!

The following list provides some tips to make your chatting experiences easier and more fruitful.

1. *Finding the correct chat room is a must.* Surf until you find one that fits your needs.

2. *Have patience with your connection*, your system, and the entire process.

3. *Set up your computer altar* and get magically prepared to chat.

4. *Turn on your favorite music.* This helps you get in the chatting mood and sets the tone.

5. *When you enter a chat room, check out what people have been saying before you entered.* Any comments that were made previous to your entry into the room are usually available by scrolling up.

6. *DON'T YELL.* Capital letters usually signify that a person is yelling or shouting. Only do so when absolutely necessary.

7. *Take turns talking.* Discussion-type chat forums have been found to be much more productive if users take turns commenting and contributing.

8. *Choose a moderator* (High Priestess, High Priest, Head Web Witch, Chief Wiccan, pagan leader) for the room. This person provides direction when needed.

9. *Prepare your comments.* The comment can be typed in advance, and when the time is right or your turn comes up, just press enter.

10. *Research the topic of the chat, if possible.* If the chat is prescheduled and publicized in advance, know what the topic is and something about it so you can really contribute. If it's a ritual, know what your part is (if any), and know who is leading the ritual and what pagan tradition they follow.

11. *Target your comment.* If you have something to ask or want to reply to a specific individual, start your sentence with that person's name.

12. *Stay focussed on the chat room theme*, topic, ritual, spell-working, etc. It's extremely frustrating to go into cyberspace expecting to talk about one thing, and then hearing about the TV shows that week!

13. *If necessary, whisper private conversations.* It's possible to send a message privately to a person through a special window in most chat rooms.

14. *Be concise.* If you get to the point quicker, there is less you will need to type.

15. *Have fun* and meet more Web Witches by exchanging e-mail addresses and Web page URLs, fun links, and other hot Web discoveries.

IRC Chat

Many chat sites use a protocol called Internet Relay Chat. This allows people to chat using sound or sound and video, depending upon whether you have the hardware and software capabilities, the bandwidth access, and so forth. It also allows you to start a chat group, channel, or join an existing channel. Certain sites on the Web such as Talk City or IRC Networks provide servers and help you download the IRC client to your PC. A client "talks" over the Internet to another computer, which acts as an IRC server. An IRC client applet is also available from Talk City. For IRC tutorials, FAQs, and a comprehensive source of information about IRC, we recommend the IRC Help Page, IRC.Net, or big.net. The Undernet offers one of the world's largest network of IRC servers.

ICQ Links and Chats

Millions of ICQ (pronounced "I seek you") users now exist around the world, with about 40 percent in the United States and 60 percent in Europe. It is an instant e-mail program that informs you when other ICQ users are online and lets you exchange instant messages with them. ICQ offers many features such as file and URL transfers, offline message composition, e-mail notification, message forwarding, multiuser chat, contact and buddy lists, excellent visual alerts, and lots of configuration options. Be sure to download the right version of ICQ for your computer platform—(PC or Mac). ICQ help pages and message boards have loads of information to simplify and clarity the process.

There are several sites on the Web that describe ICQ links with tips, tricks, and shortcuts. One of the best is the ICQ Web page at www.icq.com. Downloading ICQ and installing it into your system is easy (and free), but keep in mind that versions of ICQ are constantly being updated. For example, one of ICQ 99's new features lets you send instant voice messages or .wav (audio) files.

How to Use Message Boards

The message boards or bulletin boards of the magical community are pretty standard. Once you find a site, you can read the messages and respond to those you wish, or past a new message.

How to Stay Informed

To get information about Wiccan Web events such as chats, classes, and rituals, register for online pagan newsletters. Just type "Wiccan newsletters" into the search engine you're using (we suggest 37.com). To register, you enter your e-mail address at the site offering the newsletter. Then you automatically receive the newsletter via your e-mail whenever it's issued. You can always unsubscribe to the newsletter whenever you want.

Other ways to stay abreast of Wiccan happenings on the Web are to surf to some of the larger pagan sites such as neopagan.com, avatar.com, and triplemoon.com, and check their events or calendar listings. The site will often have a navigation bar you can click on that is labeled Upcoming Events or Calendar of Events that lists all the events for the next month or longer. We suggest you bookmark these sites as a way to stay current with what is happening on the Wiccan Web. Please see chapter 7 for specific listings.

Wiccan Networking on the Internet

Pagan cyber communities, circles, and covens are being launched every day on the Wiccan Web. This is one of the reasons the Web is such an incredible resource for pagans. Many practitioners find themselves without a local group to work with, but with the advent of the Wiccan Web, there are always fellow pagans you can connect with, either in chat rooms, pods, or Webrings.

Be sure to check out any online pagan communities before joining them. Find out who is the Webmaster or Ringmaster, what his or her background and training is, and what the intentions of the site are.

There are advantages and disadvantages to working with pagans on the Web. Some of the advantages are the fact that you can reach out globally as opposed to just locally; you don't have to clean the house for a ritual; and if you find you don't like someone, you don't have to have them in your face. The main disadvantage is that the Web is not up-close and personal, and so you can't see your fellow members smile or touch or hold hands to build up or direct magical energy. There is something very profound and magical about physical proximity, especially if you are a tactile kind of Web Witch.

As you become more adept at Web Witching and get more proficient at surfing, you will find the groups and sites that work for you. Use your magical skills and intuition to choose your fellow Web Witches.

There are several basic Wiccan group classifications online.

CIRCLE   A loosely structured group of people who gather together for the purpose of doing magic and ritual. This is the most common kind of Wiccan group on the Web, and they are mostly informal with little or no hierarchy. Learning the Craft is the responsibility of each individual member.

COVEN   A close-knit small group of women and men (usually up to thirteen members) who are lead by an elected High Priestess and High Priest. Initiation, personal training, and degree levels are often included.

GROVE   Less formal than a coven, and more loosely structured, a grove consists of many members, novices as well as those more experienced with the Craft, who enjoy Wicca for its rituals and celebrations.

POD   Pods are online member communities that are based on themes, interests, or subject areas that are shared by pod members. You can get involved in as many pods as you want and participate in pod events and chats and submit your URL for inclusion on the pod publisher's list. Pods are created and maintained by Poderators, who keep the pod updated and keep members informed of happenings, usually through a newsletter. Pods are easy to join and all have an "Add Me to This Pod" button you can click on. Tripod.com is probably the best known pod site on the Web.

WEBRING   A Webring is a group of Web pages with similar content that are linked together, usually maintained by a Ringmaster. This makes it easier to find information on certain subjects. Anyone can surf a Webring, but if you want to add your Web site to one, you must meet the qualifications of the ring. The Ringmaster will review your Web page and e-mail your acceptance. All Webrings are different, so make sure you are familiar with their submission process, rules, etc.

CLUBS   Several clubs are available on the Wiccan Web, each of them focussing on a particular topic such as shamanism, shapeshifting, sex magic, or spellworking. Sirona's club address is www.clubs. yahoo.com/sironaknight. Trish's club address is www.clubs.yahoo. com/clubs/folkmagicwithtrishtelesco.

CLAN   A clan is a large and informal group of Wiccans with similar interests and agendas who gather together primarily on the Sabbats to celebrate and share knowledge. A clan usually has an Inner and Outer Court. Most of the clan members are in the Outer Court, while the Inner Court consists of many individual covens, groves, and circles.

TRIBE   A tribe is a large, structured society made up of several clans, usually connected to a particular locale, and very often the descendants of a common deity, heroine, hero, person, coven, or clan. There is usually a tribal leader (Rix) and adviser to the leader (Druis). The entire tribe usually only gathers together for the Sabbats or once a year.

7

WICCAN WEB SITES

In assembling this section, we have done our best to keep the site listings timely, useful to the Wiccan/pagan community, and representative of positive, well-established sites that aren't likely to disappear soon. However, as you've probably already noticed, things on the Internet change very quickly. We've set up information centers at www.sironaknight.com and www.loresinger.com. At these sites you can e-mail us about new Web pages that you recommend, share any problems you experience, or let us know when a site's URL changes.

Always remember, it's just plain pagan smart to cloak yourself before surfing the Internet. Go to www.the-cloak.com and click on. It's that easy. Cloaking keeps your surfing experience a safe and private one. Cloak whenever you log on to the Internet, use search engines, go Web shopping, and during chats.

Following are some good Web sites to visit. Bear in mind this is only a very small minority of the many wonderful sites on the Wiccan Web.

SIRONA KNIGHT/BLUESKY   www.sironaknight.com and www.dcsi.
net/~bluesky/
   Author's personal site dedicated to linking creativity, spirituality,
and world peace together into one. Includes interviews with authors
and musicians, overviews and excerpts from Sirona Knight's books,
a monthly e-mail newsletter, lectures, workshops, great links, and is
updated regularly.

www.angelfire.com/sk/goldenwells/
   Author's site dedicated to the Shapeshifter Tarot deck, with
sample cards, reviews, and other information on shapeshifting.

PATRICIA TELESCO   www.loresinger.com
   A site dedicated to overviews of Trish Telesco's books, upcoming
travel plans, lectures, and a regularly updated editorial on pressing
Wiccan and pagan issues. Includes some neat graphics you can use
as your own.

Books

AMAZON.COM   www.amazon.com
Internet bookstore with a secure ordering service for credit card customers. The site includes lists of best-sellers in the area of magic, the occult, and Wicca, pictures of book covers, descriptions of each book, reviews from readers, interviews from authors, related titles, used books, and an out-of-print search service.

BARNES AND NOBLE BOOKS   www.barnesandnoble.com
Well-known chain bookstore that can be found in your local neighborhood as well as on the Web. The Web site has a secure ordering service for credit card customers. The site includes lists of best-sellers in the area of magic, the occult, and Wicca, pictures of book covers, descriptions of each book, reviews from readers, interviews from authors, related titles, and an out-of-print search service.

BLUE STAR PRODUCTIONS   www.bkworld.com
A small press specializing in the paranormal, mystical nonfiction and fiction, unfology, and spiritual fantasy.

CROSSING PRESS   www.crossingpress.com
This site offers books on Wicca. There are also weekly recipes, hot-title notes, an effective search engine, and links.

HARPERCOLLINS SAN FRANCISCO   www.harpercollins.com
An imprint specializing in spirituality and religious issues. Some great Wicca titles by Sirona, Trish, and Starhawk. Nice site for surfing, offering pictures of book covers, an alphabetical title list, and a good internal search feature.

GALDE PRESS   www.galdepress.com
This site isn't wholly dedicated to magical books, but there are a few here worth a peek, especially for those with pagan children.

INNER TRADITIONS   www.innertraditions.com
Site with New Age listings, tarot decks, some Wicca books, color covers, and a best-seller list.

KENSINGTON BOOKS, INC.   www.kensingtonbooks.com
Extensive catalog of books, both fiction and nonfiction. Great site
for surfing, and several best-selling Wicca books to choose from.

LLEWELLYN WORLDWIDE   www.llewellyn.com
This site includes links to authors, e-mail contacts within the
company, and a good internal search function. You can order a catalog and even get a free tarot reading with the Shapeshifter Tarot!

NEW PAGE BOOKS/CAREER PRESS   www.newpagebooks.com
An excellent new imprint of books on Wicca, druidism, astrology,
numerology, and spellcrafting. Great authors and great books!

SAMUEL WEISER   www.weiserbooks.com
Includes an extensive catalog of books on Wicca, shapeshifting, the
Goddess, druidism, astrology, numerology, magic, and spellcrafting.
Also has author tour schedules, links, book descriptions, and more.

STERLING PUBLISHING CO., INC.   www.sterlingbooks.com
Some Wicca books and lots of Celtic-traditions books. Check out
their gardening and aromatherapy books!

Divination Sites

DREAMPOWER TAROT ONLINE TAROT READING
www.dreampower.com
R. J. Stewart's Dreampower Tarot site. Easy to use—just click on
for a comprehensive reading. Takes a little time, but well worth it.

FACADE   www.facade.com
Comprehensive divination site with tarot, runes, I-Ching, bio-
rhythms, stichomancy, bibliomancy, and much more. You can
choose from different tarot decks for your reading.

INTERNET HOROSCOPES   www.internethoroscopes.com
This site delivers your daily horoscope to you via e-mail. Site
includes lots of excellent links.

LEARNING THE TAROT: AN ONLINE COURSE
http://learntarot.org/top.htm

Complete course on how to read tarot cards with lessons, spreads, sample readings, and samplings of lots of tarot decks.

THE MATRIX ORACLES   http://thenewage.com

A variety of interactive oracles including astrology, tarot, runes, I-Ching, numerology, fortune cookies, word oracle, free astrology screensavers, and more.

ORACLE OF CHANGES   www.iching.com

Visionary Networks' authentic interactive online readings, animated online oracle experiences, free newsletter, articles and interviews, products, and more. Definitely one of the more accurate online oracles!

TAROT MAGIC   www.tarotmagic.com

Visionary Networks' free tarot readings online. This amazing site has hundreds of tarot decks to choose from!

Festivals and Gatherings

ABOUT.COM   http://paganwiccan.about.com

Guide to pagan news, sites, current issues, Wiccan college groups, shops, publishers, humor, artists, and sacred places. Great search engine.

ASSOCIATION FOR CONSCIOUSNESS EXPLORATION (ACE)
www.rosencomet.com

Information about Starwood and other pagan festivals and events.

COUNCIL OF THE MAGICKAL ARTS (COMA)   www.magickalarts.com

Group in Texas that holds ongoing events and offers a regular magical magazine.

DRAGON HILLS   www.dragonhills.com

This site holds various festivals throughout the year.

HEARTLAND SPIRITUAL ALLIANCE AND PAGAN FESTIVAL
www.microlink.net/~shanem/home1.htm
  Home page for the Heartland Spiritual Alliance and the Heartland Pagan Festival.

PHOENIX PHYRE   www.phoenixfestivals.com
  This group organizes numerous events throughout the year, being
careful not to time them when other neighboring events are taking
place. The main site has much more to offer than simple festival
information. For specifics, see the site's pagan links.

Herbs, Gardening Information, and Supplies

ALGY'S HERB PAGE   www.algy.com/herb/index.htm
  Everything you wanted to know about growing, harvesting, and
crafting with herbs, seed exchange, medicinal uses of herbs, culi-
nary uses of herbs, and more.

ASHLYNN'S GROVE, A PAGAN INFORMATION SOURCE
http://paganism.com/ag/index2.html
  Herbal database of over 310 herbs, lots of articles, reviews, supplies, how-to information, celestial tables, a children's section, a message board, pagan classified ads, a chat room, pagan greeting cards,
graphics, links, and more.

SEEDS OF CHANGE   http://st4.yahoo.net/seedsochange
  Certified organic, 100 percent open-pollinated seeds, eco-bulbs,
organic live seedlings, organic kitchen recipes, slide shows, books,
and lots of links.

WISTERIA'S HERBAL GRIMOIRE   www.wisterias-realm.com
  Excellent site with information on herb gardens, magical gardens,
natural beauty, herbal apothecary, a herbal quick reference, and a
listing of herbs and their magical properties.

Information, Resources, Chat Rooms, and Links

Ár nDraíocht Féin   www.adf.org
Well-known druid organization. Initiation, classes, links, and lots of great information.

Berkeley Psychic Institute   http://dnai.com/~dejavu
Offers clases on psychic development. In addition, the Institute holds regular gatherings that focus on healing, meditation, and other spiritual issues. They also produce a regular journal, the *Psychic Reader*, and coordinates tours to sacred sites around the world.

Calliope's Castle   www.geocities.com/Athens/Olympus/8774/
Author Dorothy Morrison's home page; includes great links to places like AMER, CAST, Circle Sanctuary, and many more.

The Celtic Connection   http://members.tripod.com/~Diogenes_MacLugh/celtic.html
Lots of useful information on the Celts and druids, including a druidic history of the Celts. Many choice Celtic and druid links.

Celt.net   http://www.celt.net
A Web site that was established to provide an online home for the Celtic community. Lots of resources, links, organizations, and a searchable Celtic encyclopedia.

Church of All Worlds   www.caw.org
Pagan-friendly spiritual organization.

Circle Sanctuary   www.circlesanctuary.org
Circle Sanctuary has sacred land set aside for festivals throughout the year. This organization produces a magazine, offers spiritual counseling services, and much more. The site is easy to follow and provides a great deal of information about the history and beliefs of the group.

Covenant of the Goddess   www.cog.org
An international organization of Wiccan congregations and solitary practitioners. Lots of information and links.

COLLEGE AND TEMPLE OF THELEMA   www.thelema.org
Based in the Mystery Traditions, this site gives information on the classes the college offers, and its basic philosophy. The site also offers links to esoteric supplies online, event information, and the like.

CRYSTALINKS   www.crytalinks.com
A site overflowing with information and studies on sacred places, interesting teachings on ancient civilizations and mysteries like the Ark of the Covenant, and much more. Also provides links to other excellent sites.

FRIENDS OF FREEDOM   www.friendsoffreedom.com
A Rainbow virtual community site with lots of information, an events calendar, crafts, Earth-related articles and information, listings of artists, music, and vital links.

THE GUIDE TO UNBIOLOGICAL SPECIES   www.gryphonheart.com
An online bestiary of hundreds of fabulous creatures, monsters, and supernatural beings from the world of myth.

MILITARY PAGAN NETWORK   www.milpagan.org
A site dedicated to serving pagans in the military community. Provides links to military pagans, a message area, access to chat rooms, a resource center, news, events, articles, and more.

NOVA SCOTIA HIGHLAND VILLAGE SOCIETY   www.highlandvillage.ns.ca
A nonprofit charitable organization that operates the Highland Village Outdoor Pioneer Museum, Roots Cape Breton Genealogy, Family History Center, and Highland Village Gift Shop.

ORDER OF BARDS, OVATES, DRUIDS   http://druidry.org
A site that teaches about the bardic/druidic tradition through striking visual "click on" imagery and thought-provoking verse. Each phase of the learning process requires choices by the viewer. Check out this great site!

PAGAN COMMUNITY COUNCIL OF OHIO   www.netwalk.com~pcco
This site will provide you with information on the group, the events that they hold, their philosophy, and some interesting links to follow.

Pagan Links   http://users.southeast.net/~berlin/webpages
A neat alphabetized listing of handy sites for pagans and Wiccans. It includes some goods, festivals, and groups.

Pagan Paradise   www.paganparadise.com
This site has great links to pagan authors, organizations, newsletters, stores, graphics, lots of information, special pagan military handbook section, a Book of Shadows, and more.

The Pagan Parenting Page   www.jazgordon.com/pparent
Resource center for pagan parents with lots of information, chat rooms, forums, connections, and cool kid's stuff such as songs and stories, kid's software and shareware, Kid's Web Weaving, and organizations and publications for teens.

Soak.net   www.soak.net
This site lets you search state-by-state for natural hot springs in North America and the world. Lots of resources and information.

Spirit Web   www.spiritweb.org
Encyclopedia site that interprets ancient spiritual teachings within a modern context. Contains an incredible amount of information— and has a great search engine, too!

The Temple   www.teleport.com/~temple
An online spiritual community with its focus on lots of channeled material. There are book reviews, inspirational messages, and food-for-thought articles here that might interest a Wiccan.

The Tree of Life   http://phylogeny.arizona.edu/tree/phylogeny.html
Encyclopedic site that attempts to catalog and interlink knowledge about all life forms into a web of life.

Witch/Pagan Resources   www.pagansunite.com
Information resources on Pagan traditions such as Wicca and druidism, a nationwide listing of practitioners, chat rooms (four chat destinations—Java, Java Light, Active X, and HTML), message boards, interactive areas for pagan prose, stories, personals, postcards, a

member picture gallery, a mailing list, pagan sexuality, a teaching conclave, free e-mail, free banner exchange, and more! Home of the WPR Webring.

WITCHES VOICE   www.witchesvox.com
A comprehensive site dedicated to Wicca-related subjects including legal matters, beliefs, basic methodology, links to pagan authors, and much more. A very organized page with tons of information that's easy to navigate through. This site is very balanced in its presentation of materials.

WORLD PAGAN NETWORK (WPN)   www.geocities.com/athens/ aegean/8773/
Pagan links state by state and worldwide for finding contacts, rituals, chats, and meetings. Also includes extensive pagan magazine and newsletter listings throughout the world, including the United States, Britain, Australia, Europe, and Canada.

Magazines

AT THE EDGE   www.gmtnet.co.uk/indigo/edge/atehome.htm
This magazine focuses on a blend of archaeology, folklore, and myth, including paganism and geomancy. The site includes archival information, abstracts, and reviews.

CRESCENT MAGAZINE   www.crescentmagazine.com
Issues of *Crescent* magazine, products, links, resources, and more.

GREEN EGG: A JOURNAL OF AWAKENING THE EARTH   www.greenegg.org
Lots of Wicca information, back issues, contests, and reviews, plus events and announcements.

KELTRIA: JOURNAL OF DRUIDISM AND CELTIC MAGICK
www.magusbooks.com/keltria/Journal
This magazine's site is an excellent resource for pagans and includes back issues filled with great articles and lots of reviews of books and tarot decks. Also has links to many pagan authors.

LEY HUNTER JOURNAL   www.leyhunter.com
As the name implies, the *Ley Hunter* studies earth mysteries, sacred sites, and the art of geomancy. The site includes news, books, Webzines, definitions, and a guest book.

MAGICAL BLEND   www.magicalblend.com
Award-winning Web site with a reading room filled with excellent articles. The site offers a complimentary copy of the magazine, free online I-Ching readings, lots of reviews, and more.

NEOPAGAN TIMES   www.omen.com.au/~onelife/neopag/neopag.html
An online journal dedicated to neopagan philosophies and practices. It includes articles, book reviews, interviews, and links. Very clean, crisp site (no fluff, few graphics); easy to navigate and quick loading.

OBSIDIAN   www.tiac.net/users/madstone
A journal dedicated to myth, folklore, and Mystery Traditions, this site (as well as the magazine) is a veritable feast for the eyes featuring evocative color images that inspire and would make good focus points for meditation. The site is well mapped, includes links for goods and services, and you can sign up for the mailing list.

SAGE WOMAN   www.sagewoman.com/
Site for a great magazine with lots of articles and links.

STARLIGHT VOICES   http://members.tripod.com/~StarlightVoices/
A newsletter dedicated to pagan youth spirituality with pagan pals, polls, book reviews, creative writing, community news, magical spells, and crafts.

WICCAN PAGAN TIMES   www.twpt.com
A comprehensive online magazine featuring interviews with Wiccan authors, articles, editorials, news, features, happenings around the Web, book reviews, pagan links, bulletin boards, chat rooms, and more.

Music

ALAN STIVELL   www.alan-stivell.com
Famous Breton harpist's home page. Sound samples and more!

CELTIC.COM   www.celtic.com

A global Irish, Scottish, and Welsh online community. Celtic music, books, videos, free Celtic e-mail addresses, postcards, and more.

GLOBAL PACIFIC MUSIC   www.ninegates.com/global.html

Music dedicated to one-world thinking and linking the world together. This site is nice because it includes sound file samples to help you determine which CDs or tapes are best for you. There are also links, a catalogue offer, featured artists, and simple suggestions on ways we can all help heal the Earth.

LOREENA MCKENNITT   www.quinlanroad.com

Singer/songwriter Loreena McKennitt's home page.

MP3 TOP TWENTY-FIVE SITES   www.firechicken.com/top-mp3/index.shtml

Great links to MP3 sites, software, downloads, lots of music. Check it out!

MAGGIE'S MUSIC   www.maggiesmusic.com

A record label with its heart and soul in the new Celtic renaissance. Lots of titles and great selections.

MAIREID SULLIVAN   http://home.earthlink.net/~maireidsullivan

Celtic songwriter and singer Maireid Sullivan's homepage, with articles, interviews, poetry, notes, samples, reviews, and lots of great links.

NETREAL/SCOTTISH MUSIC   www.netreal.co.uk/9

A Scottish music index with a Celtic accent provided by NetReal. Culburnie Records, Shoots and Roots, Anna Murray, Corner House, Fiddle 98, Arran Folk Festival, the Chipolatas, Carnyx and Co, the Belle Star Band, Bella McNab's Dance Band, and many more.

Sacred Sites

ANCIENT BRITAIN   www.weldwood.demon.co.uk

A photo guide to the sacred sites of ancient Britain. Contains good historic information, a clickable location map, links, a directory, and site coordinates.

ANCIENT SCOTLAND   www.ehabitat.demon.co.uk/scotland/index
Similar to the photo guide to Britain except this site includes a search engine, books, links, and some pictish sites.

DIRECTORY OF ANCIENT SITES   www.henge.demon.co.uk
Another guide to UK sites with a good bibliography, mailing list, links, and glossary of terminology.

PLACES OF PEACE AND POWER   www.sacredsites.com
A site dedicated to the travels and studies of Mr. Martin Gray over fifteen years. There are circles, temples, pyramids, and pilgrimage sites in full color with accompanying histo-religious information.

Search Engines

37   http://37.com
One of the fastest, most powerful search engines that gives you results from up to thirty-seven search engines at one time. Saves a lot of headaches! Also horoscopes, weather, news, music, games, chats, stocks, movies, joke engine, and more, all at one site.

ALTAVISTA   www.altavista.com
One of the better search engines on the Web for Wiccan and pagan topics. Easy to use and lots of extras like free e-mail.

AVATAR   www.avatarsearch.com
This search engine is dedicated wholly to occult and metaphysical sites. The search engine includes some nice links, it's community funded, and it even includes a section about missing and kidnapped children. The only downside is that some of the links are a bit unsavory (on the dark side), and that a lot of folks haven't listed with them yet.

BEAUCOUP   www.beaucoup.com
Great search engine for just about anything.

DOGPILE   http://dogpile.com
A great search engine that fetches your sites for you from hundreds of different search engines and shows you summaries.

YAHOO   www.yahoo.com
One of the best search engines on the Web for the sole reason
that you can usually find what you are looking for. Lots of extras
like free e-mail.

Suppliers

ANCIENT CIRCLES   www.ancientcircles.com
Celtic jewelry, gold bermeil, sterling silver, torcs, moons, knotwork, spirals, masks, spell kits, gowns, drums, Celtic textiles, rugs,
capes, and more.

ANCIENT WAYS   www.conjure.com/aw
Books, candles, oils, herbs, a newsletter, plus links to other merchant sites.

AZURE GREEN/ABYSS   www.Azuregreen.com
A complete source for pagan books, tapes, videos, and ritual
tools. Also carries herbs, oils, candles, posters, incense, jewelry, and
many other pagan supplies.

THE BLESSED BEE   www.theblessedbee.com
Wiccan site that has supplies and pagan scholarships.

BLUE PEARL   www.bluepearlworld.com
This site sells incense, oils, stones, music, pendulums, meditation bundles, decals, and more. Full-color pictures and descriptions
of many products.

THE CELTIC HEART   www.celticheart.com
Celtic jewelry, calligraphy, books, postcards, handcrafted jewelry
made with sterling silver or 14K gold wire and gemstones. Many
styles of pendants, rings, earcuffs, hand jewelry and neckpieces. Free
shipping.

CHIVALRY SPORTS RENAISSANCE STORE   www.renstore.com
Books on Celtic culture and legends, plus costumes, armor,
swords, jewelry, and gifts.

Cool Stones—Lost Mountain Trading Company
www.coolstones.com
Some of the finest runestones available made from semiprecious gemstones. There are fourteen different kinds of stones. Also carries a large selection of Celtic jewelry, engraved runestone pendants, and silver products.

Dragon Manor Library   www.telapex.com/~graywlkr/library/index.html
A great site for finding pagan books and music, in association with Amazon.com. Reviews on many books.

Equinox   www.monmouth.com/~equinoxbooks
This site has a really good browser, a list of moon phases and holidays, and a secure ordering service.

Mystic Caravan   http://mystic-caravan.com/18
Beautiful full-color Celtic design T-shirts by Welsh artist Jen Delyth. Celtic dragons and ravens, trees of life, antlers, moons, and Kernunnos. Celtic designs inspired by mythology and folklore on sterling jewelry, silk scarves, art prints, recycled paper stationery, cards, and more.

Moonscents and Magical Blends   www.moonscents.com
A one-stop shop for wonderful incense, oils, and magical clothing. The site also includes a bunch of magical recipes, spells, meditations, helpful hints, and reading suggestions.

Salem West   www.neopagan.com
Home of the annual Real Witches Ball, this physical and online pagan store has everything practitioners need! The owner, author A. J. Drew, really supports the magical community. Great values on herbs and incense, and comprehensive online listings and bios of pagan authors, reviews of their books, and reviews on products. Ritual tools, jewelry, statuary, custom-crafted ceramics, and much more!

TRIPLEMOON WITCHWARE   www.witchware.com

The site has a complete catalog of pagan supplies, chat rooms, classes, hosted book discussions, a community directory, message boards and forums, an astrological almanac, virtual postcards with sound and custom features, and more.

www.shadowlandonline.com

Hand-carved fetishes, pottery, jewelry, kachinas, beadwork, and other native crafts.

www.blackhawksgallery.com

Hand-carved and painted gourds, custom designs, power pouches, masks, and much more.

www.waterhawkcreations.com

Athames, cups, wands, bowls, chalices, horns, scrying stones—all handmade and spiritually inspired.

APPENDIX I

How to Create Your Personal Web Page

Web sites come in all sizes, shapes, types, and topics, and exist all over the world. Besides the millions of business Web pages where people sell goods and services, there is also a treasury of personal Web pages set up by people like yourself, who generally are interested in two things: getting their ideas and messages on Wicca, paganism, magic, and other related information and teachings out there to the world; and connecting with like-minded people in a loosely structured yet supportive pagan network. Our hope is that by reading this book and applying the spells, rituals, and practical directions, you will gain the knowledge and power to do both!

This appendix is intended as a basic primer for creating your personal Web page and becoming part of the growing Wiccan Web. The information given here is basic, with an emphasis on helping you acquire the space for a Web page, create it (including design and adding graphics), and linking your Web page to other people's sites and to existing Internet pagan networks. Also provided are easy-to-follow instructions for registering your Web page with the search engines so that people can easily find you.

Acquiring Your Web Page

One of the easiest way to acquire a Web page is to purchase it as part of a package from your Internet provider. The fees vary depending on what you are getting, including how much disk space you get for your personal page. Some providers give you access to the Internet and about twenty-three megs of space for your personal Web page, all for around $20 a month. This is fairly standard; if you shop around, you can sometimes get better deals—as little as $9.95 per month for Internet access.

Another way to get personal Web page space or to be able to own more than one page is to go to one of the many sites that offer free Web page space. Some of these places include Geocities (www. geocities.com), Angelfire (www.angelfire.com), and Tripod (www. tripod.com). As long as you have an e-mail address, each of these sites will give you a free Web page just for registering with them. This is a great deal, especially when you are just starting out. When you become more familiar with Web pages, you can acquire several personal pages on different subjects and link them together, thus increasing both the amount of information you can put on the Web as well as increasing your Wiccan Web visibility.

Creating Your Web Page

Some of the places that provide free Web pages space, also include a template for setting up your home page. These are very easy to use. To design your page, you just answer the questions on the template, as the title of your page and the background and text colors you'd like. These templates are great when you are starting out, but as you become more advanced, you will want to add things that are not on the template. This can be done with a software program or by using HTML code.

Everything on the Web is written in HTML, an acronym that stands for Hypertext Markup Language. HTML is not a programming language; it evolved from early word processing programs such as WordStar. What you are seeing when you look at the HTML code of a Web page is all of the text that appears on the page, but this text is bracketed off with codes that tell the Web browser how the page should appear in terms of fonts, graphics, color, placement, and so on. HTML is like the magic words you use in spells or rituals, the thing that sets your intention and energies in place. If you are curious about how to use HTML and want to know how to use it to create your Web page, there are many Web sites available that will teach you about the codes. They are straightforward and easy to understand. Just search for "HTML code" on any search engine.

Learning HTML isn't a necessary requirement in designing your personal Web page, so don't let any past-life HTML code bugaboos keep you from getting your personal page and connecting to the Wiccan Web.

Software programs such as Microsoft Word and Corel WordPerfect offer an easy means for creating your Web page. Microsoft Word in particular lets you select one of several design templates or a blank Web page in which you can you type information and add graphics just like you would in a word processing document.

These software programs are relatively easy to use because what you see on screen is how the page is going to appear on the Web. The nice part of these programs is that they write the HTML code for you. However, in some ways your personal Web page adventure only really begins when you figure out how easy it is to use HTML code. You can do a lot more with graphics, sound, animation, and stylizing when you use HTML.

Designing Your Web Page

Your personal Web page is an extension and expression of yourself, changing as you change and evolve as a person. When designing it, the first step is to determine what it is you want to say with your page and how you want to say it. If you are a Wiccan who does rituals with a group, you might give information about your group, or share practices and personal experiences. If you follow a particular tradition, you might use the page to inform people about what your tradition is about and how others can access information about your Path. You can include information regarding a favorite goddess or god that has helped you in your spiritual quest. Your page should be a reflection of you and what you want to present to the World Wide Web, and is only limited by your imagination, HTML skills, and the memory available to host your page. On Geocities, you are given unlimited space to express yourself, so be creative and connect to the Cyber god and goddess within you. You can even use your Web page to share recipes, pet photos, the best places to find Pagan supplies, and information on seeds, plants, and supplies for growing a magical garden.

Before you begin designing your Web page, it's a good idea to surf the Internet and check out other people's Web pages and how they are put together. Some people put everything on one main page, and others use a main start-up page that includes a menu. Each item on the menu is a hyperlink that sends Web surfers to other documents within the same page.

Hyperlinks are very easy to create, especially when using Microsoft Word. All you do is highlight the menu selection, choose "hyperlink" from the Insert menu, and when it prompts you for the destination, type in the name of the file you want to jump to.

Remember that your Web page will be in a constant state of evolution, so it's okay to start out with everything on one main page; you can always separate it out into different documents later as you become more familiar with Web design.

Adding Graphics and Photos to Your Web Page

Graphics and photos are elements that help to lend character to a Web page. There are many places to get artwork, photos, and clips that you can import into your personal Web page. The first place to begin is with the software program you use to create your page; most come with an assortment of clip art. Beyond that, there are CD-roms available that have a wide variety of graphics on them.

One of things Sirona bought when she was starting out, was a booklet and CD of Celtic art. I imported the images from the CD into her Web page, and placed them where she wanted them. One of the best places to get graphics for your Web page is from the Internet itself. There are many sites that offer both free images and for-purchase graphics. Just make sure that when you use art off of the Internet you are not committing copyright infringement. If you like a particular graphic, e-mail the person who owns the page and ask where he or she got the graphic and if you can use it on your page.

If you own a scanner or have access to one, you can add your own pictures and photos to your Web page. Graphics software programs such as Photoshop allow you to scan the photo, crop it, add special effects, and generally personalize the image. Make sure you save the picture as either a .gif or .jpeg file. Then you can import the photo into your Web document.

Other things you can add to your site are a counter (for counting how many people visit your site) and a guest book (so people can sign in and give you feedback regarding your page). Several Web sites offer free counters and guest books. Use a search engine to find the current addresses of these sites. Usually they give you the code for the counter and/or guest book, which you then copy and paste into your page.

Linking to Other Wiccan Web Sites

The reason it is called the World Wide Web is because it is essentially a bunch of servers and sites linked together into something resembling a spider's web. The individual links make the Web what it is as a whole. Because of this, it is important to link your page to other pages. This way the circle becomes stronger!

One of the easiest ways to establish links is to surf the Internet. When you find a site you like, add it to your links. Let the Webmaster of the site you have added know you have done so by e-mailing him or her. You can also request that they add your site to *their* links page. People are usually quite agreeable to these types of cross-links because it brings more people into both sites.

Another link that you might want to include on your personal Web page is a hyperlink to your e-mail address, which allows people to e-mail you simply by clicking on the text or graphic. Setting this up is easy. Begin by highlighting the text or graphic you want people to click on in order to send a message to you. Next, insert the hyperlink (in Microsoft Word this is done under the "insert" menu). When the program prompts you for an address, type in mailto: followed by your e-mail address.

Registering Your Web Page With Directories and Search Engines

One of the best ways to get people to visit your Web page is to register it with the various directories and search engines on the Web. Yahoo is one of more well-known directories, and registering with them is a matter of finding the category that best describes your page, for example, "New Age/Wicca/Divination." Once you have found the category in which your site belongs, then click the icon that will allow you to register your site. Generally, you'll have to answer a list of questions about your site that will give the search engine provider information as to what your site is about.

Search engines such as AltaVista, Hotbot, Lycos, and Excite, can use different criteria in evaluating and listing your site. Some engines use what are known as metatags, which are codes in the HTML listed between the title and body of your document, which again, tell the search engine what your site is about. In addition, search engines use programs known as "spiders" to quickly evaluate the content of your personal Web page. Depending on what the spiders tell them and the evaluation criteria they use, the search engines then list your site accordingly. Sometimes it can be frustrating to get your site listed by the search engines, but we have found they eventually list you if you try different things such as changing your metatags (check out www.webgarage.com for more information on your metatags), or resubmitting your page to the search engines. Be patient! Most engines take a couple of weeks to list your page. There are also many sites that say they will register your site with the search engines in exchange for you displaying their banner on your Web page. My experience has been that some of these do what they promise and some don't. Some sites allow you to submit to several sites at once for free, like www.submitit.com.

APPENDIX II

WEB RESOURCES

One of the best things about the Web is its potential as a source of information. Thirty years ago, very few of us realized how much information and how many people could be right at your fingertips, the equivalent of a phone call away. In fact, back then the Web was closer to science fiction than science fact. Yet today, by logging on you can access a variety of information sources that include the Library of Congress, medieval history resources, and Wiccan sites. The following is an overview of informational sites that you can visit as well as suggestions for finding whatever you want on the Wiccan Web.

For general information, several sites offer extensive resources for finding just about anything that you have an interest in. One is the Library of Congress (lcweb.loc.gov/harvest/), which connects you into a database that includes a listing for nearly every book published in the United States. Another online library is the Vassar College Libraries at www.iberia.vassar.edu/vcl//electronics/etc/subject. html, which offers an extensive amount of information from one of the better libraries in the country. Another great source is the Encyclopedic Theosophical Glossary at www.theosociety.org/pasadena/ etgloss/etg-hp.htm. If you are looking for an online encyclopedia, www.encyclopedia.com/ is free and contains all the information from *The Concise Columbia Electronic Encyclopedia, 3rd Edition.*

Two resources for medieval information are the Online Medieval and Classical Library (sunsite.berkeley.edu/OMACL/) and the Labyrinth, sponsored by Georgetown University (georgetown.edu/labyrinth/labyrinth-home.html). Through these kinds of sites the Web connects the past, present, and future together into one. In the process, technology meets tradition, both complementing, rather than competing with, each other.

A fascinating site that I happened upon recently was Treehuggers (www.afn.org/~afn49740/), billing itself as Web resources for social, political, and spiritual liberals. They have sections on Wicca and neopaganism, including a listing of sites for connecting with like-minded individuals. As with many Web resources, it offers a stepping-stone to many other Web adventures and in the process, connections with interesting people. This and the other sites listed earlier are meant as starting points to guide you along your way along the Wiccan Web.

GLOSSARY

AOL The standard abbreviation for America Online, one of the more popular internet providers

Authentication The process that the host system uses to make sure you are who you say you are. Sometimes called the password authentication protocol, this will require giving your user name and password whenever you log on to your Internet provider. Some systems allow you to set this up as a default so the information automatically gets provided to the server.

BBS The accepted abbreviation for Bulletin Board System. You do not need anything other than hyperterminal access to post something here. Think of this like the public bulletin boards at the supermarket, only via computer, and you've got the idea.

Browser A program that lets you look at documents on the Web. Microsoft Internet Explorer is an example of a browser.

CPU Short for Central Processing Unit, this is the brain of your computer. If your CPU dies, it will take more than magic to fix the problem.

Dial-Up Network This is the program that allows you to use a local telephone line to connect with your Internet server. The dial-up includes authentication as part of the process.

DNS This stands for Domain Name Service. It allows a person or organization to have a special name associated with their Web site so that you can find them more easily. It's sort of like the online postal service, but faster.

Download Taking a file off the Internet and bringing it into your computer.

EXE A file extension that indicates this file is executable.

FAQ The abbreviation for Frequently Asked Questions. These appear on many Web sites to decrease e-mail overloads that come from people

163

asking the same questions over and over again. FAQs are very helpful in determining if a newsgroup is one you'd like to frequent.

Flame   An Internet no-no. Flames are nasty, defamatory, rude, crude, e-mail messages. This type of Internet use goes directly against netiquette.

Freenet   An Internet provider that offers its network for free as a community service.

FTP   The accepted abbreviation for File Transfer Protocol; this allows you to transmit files from one host to another.

GIF   A file extension indicating a graphics image in Graphics Image Format (this is one of the easiest for most systems to download and read).

Home Page   When you vist a Web site, the first image you see is the home page.

HTML   Hyper Text Markup Language; the most common programming language of the Net.

Icons   These are neat little images and words (sometimes flashing, highlighted, or animated) that help you navigate through a site. They indicate what areas are available to you and act like guideposts to reaching the information you most need. Watch especially for icons that say "site index" or something similar if you want a complete overview of the site.

Internet Address   This is how people reach each other on the Net. Your Internet address indicates a "who" and a "where." For example, trish@loresinger.com or bluesky@dcsi.net, indicates you'll reach Trish or Sirona through their servers at loresinger.com and dcsi.net (the domain names).

JPEG   (Also sometimes JPG) Another file extension for a graphic.

Mailing List   This works like any common mailing list, only you'll receive the material you've signed up for via e-mail. Many sites offer these for free; all you need do is click on the "mailing list" icon and fill out the information. You can also unsubscribe to these lists if you find they're not useful by e-mailing back with "unsubscribe" or "remove" as your subject line.

Moderator   In message boards and newsgroups the moderator keeps an eye on incoming submissions to make sure they're on topic, antiflame, and antispam. While moderate boards may take more time to show a message, they also save you a lot of time by not having to wade through junk to find what you want.

MPG   A file extension indicating a video-type file (includes moving images).

Netiquette   Acceptable Internet conduct. Flaming, using graphics without permission, and sending spam are not acceptable.

Shareware   Software that you can download from the Net for free. Warning: This is one way that your computer can be exposed to viruses, so scan everything with your antivirus software first. Also note that some shareware is designed to work only for a period of time, after which you must pay to get the full-blown version.

Signature Lines   A place at the end of your e-mail where you can put favorite sayings, a personal logo, and so on.

Spam   The bane of all Internet users, spam is junk e-mail. Some spam goes to individual users, while other types get posted to numerous newsgroups at the same time.

TXT   A file extension indicating a text file. DOS text or ASKII are two of the universals that allow anyone to see and read the document you're sending.

URL   The address of a website that appears in your browser address window when you're in the site (or in a specific part of a site). Giving people a URL (universal resource locator) creates a link so they can go directly to a page.

WWW   The abbreviation for World Wide Web. Most Internet addresses begin with www.

ZIP   A file extension indicating a large file that's been condensed using a program such as WinZip.

BIBLIOGRAPHY

Bowes, Susan. *Notions and Potions.* New York: Sterling Publishing, 1997.

Dvorak, John. *Dvorak's Guide to PC Telecommunications.* New York: Bantam, 1992.

Gannon, Linda. *Creating Fairy Garden Fragrances.* Pownal, Vt.: Storey Books, 1998.

Goldstein, Nikki. *Essential Energy: A Guide to Aromatherapy and and Essential Oils.* New York: Warner Books, 1997.

Heath, Maya. *Cerridwen's Handbook of Incense, Oils, and Candles.* San Antonio, Tex. Words of Wizdom International, 1996.

Knight, Sirona. *Celtic Traditions.* Secaucus, N.J.: Citadel Press, 2000.

Knight, Sirona. *Love, Sex, and Magick.* Secaucus, N.J.: Citadel Press, 2000.

Knight, Sirona. *The Pocket Guide to Celtic Spirituality.* Freedom, Calif.: Crossing Press, 1998.

Knight, Sirona. *The Pocket Guide to Crystals and Gemstones.* Freedom, Calif.: Crossing Press, 1998.

Knight, Sirona, et al. *The Shapeshifter Tarot.* St. Paul, Min.: Llewellyn Publications, 1998.

Lin, Jami. *Earth Design: The Added Dimension.* Miami Shores, Fla.: Earth Design Inc., 1995.

Nelson, Steven. *Field Guide to the Internet.* Redmond, Wa.: Microsoft Press, 1995.

Pajeon, Kala and Ketz. *The Candle Magick Workbook.* Secaucus, N.J.: Citadel Press, 1991.

Rector-Page, Linda. *Healthy Healing.* Sonoma, Calif.: Healthy Healing Publications, 1992.

Sherman, Aliza. *Cybergrrl: A Woman's Guide to the World Wide Web.*

Telesco, Patricia. *Advanced Wicca.* Secaucus, N.J.: Citadel Press, 2000.

Telesco, Patricia. *Futuretelling: A Complete Guide to Divination*. Freedom, Cal.: Crossing Press, 1998.

Telesco, Patricia. *Goddess in My Pocket*. San Francisco: HarperCollins San Francisco, 1998.

Telesco, Patricia. *The Herbal Arts*. Secaucus, N.J.: Citadel Press, 1998.

Telesco, Patricia. *The Little Book of Love Magic*. Freedom, Calif.: Crossing Press, 1999.

Telesco, Patricia. *Magic Made Easy*. San Francisco: HarperCollins San Francisco, 1999.

Telesco, Patricia. *Spinning Spells, Weaving Wonders*. Freedom, Calif.: Crossing Press, Inc., 1996.

Telesco, Patricia. *Wishing Well*. Freedom, Calif.: Crossing Press, Inc., 1997.

Tierra, Michael. *The Way of Herbs*. Santa Cruz, Calif.: Unity Press, 1980.

Vogel, Marcel. *The Crystal Workbook*. San Jose, Calif.: PRI Institute, 1986.

Williams, David and Kate West. *Born in Albion: The Re-Birth of the Craft*. Runcorn, United Kingdom: Pagan Media Ltd., 1996.

Worwood, Valerie. *The Complete Book of Essential Oils and Aromatherapy*. New York: New World Library, 1995.

INDEX